133.42
G
Garden, Nancy

Devils and demons

5.95

DATE DUE			
MAY 19 77	JUN 04	DEC 2 '9	FEB 04
1978	JUN 07	MAR 10 '92	DEC 16
NOV 7 '80	JUN 08	NOV 25	OC 14
MAY 6 '80	mllett	JUN 4 '9	DE 19 06
15	08 '86		OC 3 1
NOV 7	2 '87	OCT 22 '9	
1	FEB 29 '88	JAN 12 '9	
DEC 23	NOV 30 '88	MAY 9 '9	
MAR 26 '82	MAR 9 '89	FEB 27 '95	
APR 26	MAY 1 '91	MAY 1 '95	
JUN 03	OCT 10 '91	MAR 18 '9	
		NOV 8 '99	

Devils
and
Demons

THE WEIRD AND HORRIBLE LIBRARY

Other titles sure to chill and thrill you:

Devils and Demons

Nancy Garden

J. B. LIPPINCOTT COMPANY
PHILADELPHIA AND NEW YORK

The list on page 16 is from a cuneiform text in the British Museum, London, England, as it appeared in *Semitic* by Stephen Herbert Langdon, Volume V of the series The Mythology of All Races, Canon John Arnott MacCulloch, editor. Copyright 1931 by Marshall Jones Co., renewed 1959 by Macmillan Publishing Co., Inc. Used by permission.

The quotes on pages 13 and 100 are from *The Treasury of Witchcraft* by Harry E. Wedeck, Philosophical Library, 1961. Used by permission.

The pictures on pages 14, 19, 38, 42, 48, 55, 62, 64, 65, 70, 112, 114, 117, 124, 133, 139, and 141 were used by permission from *Devils, Demons, Death and Damnation* by Ernst and Johanna Lehner, published by Dover Publications, Inc., in 1971. The pictures on pages 22 and 104 were used by permission from *Magic, Supernaturalism and Religion* by Kurt Seligman, published by Pantheon Books, a Division of Random House, Inc. The picture on page 120 is reproduced by permission of the British Library Board.

U.S. Library of Congress Cataloging in Publication Data

Garden, Nancy.
   Devils and demons.

   (The Weird and horrible library)
   Bibliography: p.
   Includes index.
   SUMMARY: A survey of the origins and development of the belief in devils and demons.
   1. Demonology—Juvenile literature. [1. Demonology. 2. Devil] I. Title.
BF1531.G37   133.4'2   75-44461
ISBN-0-397-31666-6 ISBN-0-397-31667-4 (pbk.)

TO BARB AND WIN

WITH LOVE

Contents

Foreword

WHAT DO YOU THINK of when you hear the word *devil*?

A gruesome-looking man in red with horns, a pointed tail, and hooves instead of feet?

The serpent who tempted Eve in the Garden of Eden?

A well-dressed, witty gambler who rolls dice for human souls?

The leader of the witches at Halloween revels?

What about when you hear the word *demon*? Do you think of ancient many-headed monsters, bringers of disease and death, of war and strife? Do you think of ugly guardians of vast uncounted treasure? Of ghostly bringers of bad dreams? Of beautiful "women" who chase after men only to turn into horrible monsters—or of "men" who do the same to women? Or do you think of a certain famous demon in a certain famous movie who took over the body of a girl named Regan, causing her to do and say terrible things till the exorcist came and drove him away?

Or do you think of none of these things at all? Perhaps you say, "Nonsense, there's no such thing as a devil, or a demon either, except in people's imaginations."

That may be so. But there are people who would disagree even in this modern scientific age. Even though many, many people believe that there's no such thing as a devil or a demon, the fact remains that at all times in history, in all parts of the world, people have believed in devils or demons or both. One of the obvious questions that raises is "Why?" and, as you might expect, that isn't easy to answer.

In a way, asking why people throughout history have believed in devils and demons is like asking why people throughout history have believed in gods. A deeply religious person might say that people have always believed in gods or in a god because deities—or one deity—really exist. The same person might say the same thing about devils and demons, with just about the same explanation. But a person who felt differently about religion might say that people have believed in gods and devils because they have always needed to believe in powers stronger than themselves.

Certainly people have always had a need to explain and understand the world around them:

Why does it rain?

Why does the sun rise in the morning and set at night?

Why do people die?

Why do crops fail?

At some point early in human history, people began believing that their world was controlled by spirits something like themselves but more powerful, who were responsible for all "unexplainable" events. These spirits were the earliest gods. Some of them were in charge of good things like love and plants and good food. Others were in charge of things that could be either bad or good—the sun, for example, which was good when it helped crops grow but bad when it withered them. And still other gods were in charge of things usually considered bad. It isn't clear exactly where demons fit into this arrangement, but usually it was they who caused disease and various small annoyances like hunger and cold.

In order to prevent the "bad" gods from exerting their power, people worshiped them in much the same way that they worshiped the "good" gods. Worship in those days was a little like bribery: if we worship you, you must promise, if you're a good god, to help us. If you're a bad god, you must promise not to hurt us.

People of later religions, especially of religions that worshiped only one god, found it hard to believe that a creature in charge of evil could be a god. Therefore, these people usually referred to ancient "bad" gods as devils or demons, even though they were still considered gods by the people who worshiped them. Another factor that contributed to the mixing up of ancient gods and ancient demons was religious rivalry. As people became more aware of one another's beliefs and more puzzled by them, those who followed one religion sometimes said that the gods of other religions were really demons.

Because of this confusion, it is sometimes hard even today to distinguish between gods and demons. The most obvious starting point is to say that a god does good things and a demon does bad ones. But that doesn't always work. The Hindu goddess Kali, for example, was extremely bloodthirsty and was considered demonic by some people. But she was nonetheless considered a goddess by those who worshiped her. The ancient Greek god Pan, a goatlike being with a tail, horns, and hooves who played the pipes and danced merrily in the woods, was considered a devil by the early Christians—and many scholars think that the appearance of the Judeo-Christian Devil, Satan, was based on what Pan looked like. The ancient Romans believed that mentally ill people were victims of a goddess—not a devil—called Mania (whose name we have borrowed for our words *mania, maniac,* and *maniacal*)—but in later times it was demons who were blamed for insanity. The word for demon in Greek—*daemon*—meant a good spirit as well as an evil one. Arabian demons—*djinn,* or genies—could be either good or evil. Some Hindu demons were gods in ancient Persia. . . .

But we're going too fast! Quickly, before more demons and gods, gods and demons, demand to be mentioned, let us begin.

1

The Terrible Seven and Other Ancient Demons

THEY ARE SEVEN! They are seven!
In the depths of the ocean, they are seven!
In the brilliancy of the heavens, they are seven!
They proceed from the ocean depths, from the hidden
    retreat.
They are neither male nor female, those which stretch
    themselves out like chains; they have no spouse, they
    do not produce children; they are strangers to benev-
    olence.
The enemies! The enemies!
They are seven! They are seven! They are twice seven!
                            from an Akkadian magic tablet

These "seven" demons—for of course demons are the subject of
that magic formula—are among the most ancient and horrifying in
the world. People who lived in the Fertile Crescent of the Near East
many centuries before the birth of Christ trembled at the very
thought of them. The names and characteristics of the Seven
changed slightly as ancient civilizations rose and fell, but essentially
they remained the same for centuries. The Akkadians, whose country was part of ancient Mesopotamia, called them maskim; we will
too. The Akkadians said they lived in Arallû, which means "great

city" and which, like hell, was thought to be an underground place where people's souls went after death. Arallû was ruled by a queen named Allatu, whose son and messenger, Namtaru, commanded the maskim and any other demons who happened to be around; he was a terrible demon himself. If people prayed to their dead ancestors and made the required offerings to Namtaru, he would keep his demons away from them—but if they did not, he unleashed them full force.

Of all the demons Namtaru might unleash, the most terrible were the maskim. They were said to be invisible, but people who made

A lion-headed, eagle-footed Assyrian-Babylonian demon of disease and evil. After a wall carving at Nineveh.

carvings of them often showed them with human bodies and animal heads. One old Babylonian plaque showed them as a panther, a dog, a lion, a bird, a sheep, a wild ram, and a snake. Another showed them as a fox, a wolf, an antelope, a snake, a bird, a panther, and a wild ram; various texts refer to them as still other animals. Sometimes they were called giants, and sometimes evil gods or the messengers of the god Anu, their father. One text called them "bitter poison sent by the gods." They were also called "makers of trouble," and sometimes they were even called storms or winds. Everyone agreed that they were terrible, but no one, apparently, was able to pinpoint exactly *what* they were: giants? panthers and snakes? winds? Or were they all those things at different times? Or even all of them at the same time? We'll probably never know for sure. We can't even be sure that their number was precisely seven, for some ancient texts speak of twelve horrible demons, and most say their number is "seven times seven" as well as seven. It is possible that the maskim were too numerous to count and that the number seven was used simply because in those days it was considered magical, especially in spells.

It certainly was good to have as many spells against the maskim as possible, for these demons thought nothing of committing murder or making people sick or driving them insane. They were democratic demons in that they hurt "both the free man and the slave," according to one old tablet, and caused destruction in "the town as well as the country." Their usual trick was to lie in wait for their victims in lonely places and spring out to attack them, but they could also cause earthquakes and control the movement of the stars. In fact, the Terrible Seven could go almost anywhere and do almost anything. People in ancient times, after all, had very little understanding of natural phenomena like the phases of the moon or storms or diseases. It's very hard to live in a world where terrible things seem to happen for no reason at all. In their struggle to understand their surroundings, people in the ancient world hit on demons as an explanation for the unexplainable. Diseases, storms, unpleasant feelings like hunger and being too hot or too cold were a little easier to cope with if they had some reason for existing—so anything disastrous, strange, or scary, anything uncomfortable, unpleasant, or mysterious was apt to have a demon connected with it.

In some ancient inscriptions the demons are given separate names and assigned individual roles. Because of the wording of the inscriptions, and because the names and roles don't always add up to seven, it's not clear whether the names refer to individual demons or to groups—but regardless of their number, what they could do to a person was enough to chill anyone's blood. Here's what would probably happen if all the demons attacked at once: One, a demon called an Utukku, would grab you by the shoulder, while an Alû would make for your chest and a Gallû would seize one or both hands. An Etimmu would attack your bowels. A demon or a group of demons called Asakku would go for your head, and Namtaru—yes, the Queen's messenger himself—would take your throat.

This makes a gory picture when you think of it as all happening at once, but it's possible that multiple attacks rarely occurred. As a matter of fact, the inscription may simply mean that each demon or group of demons was responsible for diseases of a particular part of the body. A person with a headache, for example, might think he or she was being attacked by Asakku, while someone with a sore shoulder would probably blame the pain on an Utukku.

A list from the ancient land of Sumer, conquered by the Akkadians, breaks the Seven down this way:

The wicked Utukku, who slays man alive on the plain.
The wicked Alû, who covers [man] like a garment.
The wicked Etimmu, the wicked Gallû, who bind the body.
The Lamme, the Lammea, who cause disease in the body.
The Lilû, who wanders in the plain.

Because they were responsible for everyday occurrences like

diseases and storms, demons in the ancient world, however horrible, were probably accepted as a normal part of life and not thought of as unusually evil, the way demons were later. Good and evil in those days, according to some scholars anyway, were probably not considered separate forces. Even so, people of course preferred not to get sick or to be seized by the Seven "on the plains"—and so they did everything they could to protect themselves against demons.

In addition to praying and making offerings to Namtaru, you could keep the Seven away by reciting incantations like the one at the beginning of this chapter. You could also do the same thing by copying down the names of the demons and keeping the names nearby. In those days (and later also) it was believed that if you knew the name of something you would be able to control it. Therefore, any demon who saw that someone had its name written down would stay away from that person. The Assyrians, seven centuries before the birth of Christ, believed that there was one powerful name which, if spoken, could control everything in the world and in heaven and hell. Both gods and demons had to obey it. The only being who knew the name, however, was the god Ea, and he must have used it sparingly if at all, since the demons remained such an ever-present problem.

Ea had a son named Marduk whom people called on for help against the Seven; some people kept statues of him in their homes so he would protect them. According to one ancient legend, Marduk was effective against the Seven because Ea had once sent him to fight them. Even though Marduk apparently wasn't able to destroy them altogether, he must have done them some damage, for he was considered an expert demon fighter from then on. People relied on him especially when the moon was dark at the end of each month—the time when the Seven were at the peak of their power.

Of the Terrible Seven, one of the most feared was the female demon or group of demons whom the Sumerians called the Lamme. You'll remember that the Lamme is blamed for causing "disease in the body." The Lamme did a lot more than that. She was a vampirelike demon who especially enjoyed killing babies and children and drinking their blood. For that reason, she was feared greatly by women in childbirth. She also liked grown-ups' blood, however—and their flesh, after she'd drained them dry. One of her pet tricks was tying up people's muscles so they couldn't move; another was withering trees. Lamme was sometimes called "she that kindles a fire," probably because she caused terrible fevers. The Babylonians recited no fewer than thirteen incantations to get rid of her when she attacked, and the Assyrians added a ritual after each one. According to the incantations, Lamme had seven names, including besides "she that kindles a fire," "she whose face is horrible," and "sword which shatters the head." She has also been called "the seven witches."

Lamme has been described as having a bird's head, as being a cow with wings, a wolf, a cyclone, and even as being Asakku, the head-grabbing demon in one list of the Seven. Not surprisingly, if you remember the long-standing confusion between gods and demons, Lamme was also called an "angry, raging goddess."

In Babylonia, one of Lamme's close associates was a demon named Pazuzu. Pazuzu, who was sometimes called a god, was in charge of winds and wind demons. This made him a disease demon, because in those days many people thought it was the wind that spread sickness from one person to another.

Pazuzu isn't as scary a demon as many, even though he's often pictured as a very strange-looking mishmash—a combination of dog, bird, human, and scorpion. He was sometimes called "Southwest Wind," perhaps because that was the wind he best liked to ride on. To keep your house from blowing down in a bad storm, it was a good idea to hang up a little statue of Pazuzu—funny-looking though that statue might be!

Over in Egypt at around the same time, people also believed in the Terrible Seven, only there it was thought that they had come

Demons made of parts of various animals. From an illustration by Hans Holbein the Younger.

from the eyes of the god Set, along with everything else that was bad. The Egyptians used incantations to keep demons and other evil spirits from entering their bodies and causing disease; they also used protective charms. One of these was the scarab, a carved replica of their sacred dung beetle.

The true names of Egyptian demons were kept secret from most living people, but they were recorded by priests in the Book of the Dead, a collection of information believed to be useful to souls when they went to the underworld after their bodies had died. When they learned the true demonic names, of course, the dead would be able to control the demons themselves if they met them on their journey.

Most Egyptian demons were skinny, but one of the most famous, Typhon, was fat. At first the name Typhon was probably just another name for the evil god Set. But eventually people decided a separate demon must be to blame for the hot desert winds that they thought brought droughts and withered crops. They gave the name Typhon to their new wind demon, a plump winged creature usually shown with three heads and snakes for legs. Typhon appeared in Greek mythology as a hundred-headed monster, and some scholars think that much later Christians used him as one of their models for Satan. Now, of course, we use a word like his name to refer to hurricanes in or near the China Sea—*typhoons.*

Speaking of words, our word *demon* probably comes from an ancient Greek word, *daemon,* originally used to refer to a special kind of spirit who lived in the air and was halfway between a god and a human being. These spirits carried messages from the gods to humans, as did angels in later religions. Some people believed that each person had his or her very own daemon who acted more or less in the same way as did guardian angels later.

Daemons did bad things—caused disease, for example—as well as good ones. Still, it wasn't until a few hundred years before the birth of Christ that people began separating the ideas of good and evil enough to say that some daemons were exclusively evil and others were exclusively good. After Christ's birth, his followers in Greece decided *all* daemons must be evil since, like the ancient gods, they were rivals to their own god. That is probably why today we use the word *demon* to refer only to an evil being.

Nevertheless, Greece did have its share of creatures evil enough for us to call them demons today. The best known of these were probably the Lamiae. These nasty creatures were named after a queen of Libya, Lamia, who, according to legend, bore children to the god Zeus. Zeus' wife, Hera, was understandably jealous and killed Lamia's children when she found out. Then Lamia, equally jealous and terribly hurt, started stealing other women's children in revenge. Like the Lamme of the Fertile Crescent, to whom she was similar, she sucked their blood and ripped open their flesh. In time, her brutal deeds changed her from a beautiful woman to a hideous hag.

The group of demons named for this sad queen were part woman and part animal, but they could turn themselves into beauties, women as lovely as the original queen. In Greece, it was the Lamiae who stole the milk of nursing mothers. Sometimes, when she wasn't concentrating on mothers and babies, a Lamia would make a mortal man fall in love with her. Once he was in her clutches, however, she would revert to type and gobble him up.

In the meantime, while the Greeks were worried about child-stealing demons, a people called the Ammonites, who lived in what is now Jordan, were sacrificing their children to the god Moloch. Moloch is a perfect example of an ancient god who later "turned into" a demon.

To understand this, you first have to understand about human sacrifice, especially the sacrifice of children, which sounds like a horrible thing. It *is* horrible to us, but to the people who did it, it meant just what the word *sacrifice* itself means: the giving up of something you love to prove to your god how much you love and respect him and to make sure he will protect your entire tribe, not just one or two people. Moloch was probably a sun god, and the Ammonites, with a certain amount of accuracy, believed that all life comes from the sun. Children, they thought, were the most wonderful of all living things. By giving up children to Moloch the Ammonites felt they were returning to their god a portion of his most valuable gift to them. They did this for two reasons: to show their appreciation and to ensure that Moloch would not harm them. Moloch, like most powerful gods, could do evil as well as good. He could, for example, cause diseases. The sacrifice of a few children,

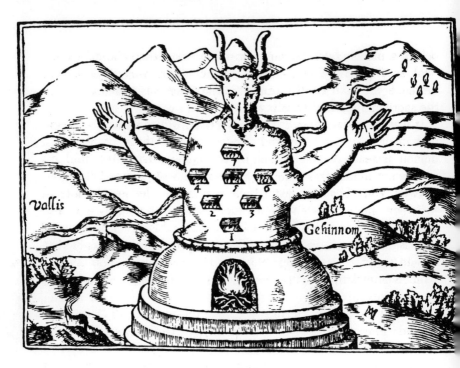

Moloch

thought the Ammonites, was not too great a price to pay to ensure the well-being of their entire people.

Moloch was a very popular god. He was probably related to a fertility god called Baal, who was worshiped by so many different tribes in the area around Palestine that there were a number of gods patterned after him, each slightly different from the others. As a group, all these gods were lumped together under the plural name Baalim. Moloch was probably one of the Baalim, the Ammonite version of Baal.

For hundreds of years, firstborn children were sacrificed to Moloch in a place called Tophet. Have you ever heard the expression "hot as Tophet"? The statue of Moloch there was an enormous bronze figure with a calf's head. In its stomach was a furnace where the sacrificial victims were burned.

It was those sacrifices that finally ended Moloch's days as a god and made outsiders who didn't worship him think of him as a demon instead. Moses, leader of the ancient Israelites, told his people not to sacrifice to Moloch, but for a while some of them did anyway. King Solomon, who built the famous Jewish Temple at Jerusalem and who was king of Israel in the tenth century B.C., also built a temple to Moloch, probably to please his Ammonite wives. But as time went on, more and more people felt strongly that human sacrifice was wrong. Bloody gods like Moloch then became symbols of evil and cruelty instead of powerful deities to be looked up to in awe.

Most of the ancient Hebrews, unlike the majority of the people around them, believed in only one god. Nonetheless, they also believed in a number of evil spirits. Many of these were similar to the demons of the Fertile Crescent, which makes sense, for the Jews were exiled in Babylonia for nearly fifty years. The shedim, for example, were probably derived from the Terrible Seven and also from another group of Babylonian demons who looked like winged bulls and were male versions of the Lamme. Some early Semitic peoples in the land of Canaan made sacrifices to the shedim as the servants of Moloch and called on them for protection against evil.

Another group of early Hebrew demons were the seirim, the "hairy ones." They looked something like the satyrs of ancient Greece (woods gods who, like their leader Pan, were part man and part goat).

Still another group of Hebrew demons were the Rephaim or Nephilim, who were a bit like the Etimmu of the Fertile Crescent, demons who were sometimes listed among the Seven and sometimes said to be the wicked souls living in Arallû. The Rephaim were giants—in fact, one was so big his bed was supposedly fifteen feet long and almost seven feet wide!

Some scholars say the Rephaim were dead souls, as the Etimmu may have been, but others say they were the children of mortal women and angelic beings who came down to earth. The origin of the shedim has been described the same way, although they have also been called the children of Eve. . . .

And that means we are moving out of ancient times into a later era, an era that saw the "birth" of Satan and other devil chiefs like him.

2
Satan and Other Devil Chiefs

LONG, LONG AGO, goes an old story, in the mountains near a little Alpine town, Satan, the chief devil in hell, and an angel of heaven held a public debate. The topic: should people follow God's teachings or Satan's? Each of the two stood in a pulpit balanced on the craggy rock walls of a green valley, and the good townspeople, most of them woodcutters, gathered eagerly around to listen.

The two argued long and cleverly, each trying hard to convince the audience that his way of life was best. Satan had always been known as a persuasive speaker but, despite his skill, one by one the woodcutters moved closer to the angel's pulpit, showing their support for his position. At last everyone was on the angel's side except those few people, mostly witches and moneylenders, who had been on the Devil's before the debate began.

Satan's voice got louder and louder and his eyes snapped fire, but at last he stopped speaking. In a tremendous fury, he seized great chunks of rock in his bare hands and heaved them up to the very top of the mountain; ever afterward the heap of rock he made was called Devil's Mill by the inhabitants of the valley. The Devil's poor sportsmanship made God just about as angry as Satan had been, and so he threw Satan down off the mountain—Lord's Meadow, the people named the place where he landed. There, say the woodcutters, you can see great gouges in the rocks made by the Devil's claws as he struggled to escape. Every time the valley is buffeted by a bad storm, they say, you can hear the Devil groaning.

This story, of course, was told long after the days when the Fertile Crescent demons flourished, and long after the birth of Christ and the beginning of Christianity. You can tell that, by the time it was told, people had a definite idea that good and evil were two separate forces and that good was represented by God and evil by Satan, or the Devil.

The idea that good and evil are two separate forces, usually called dualism, was originally developed in ancient Persia (now Iran) in the sixth or seventh century B.C. Dualism came from a religion called Zoroastrianism, named after its founder, Zoroaster. Zoroaster taught that there was a good spirit, named Ormazd or Ahura Mazda, king of light, who was constantly in battle against an evil spirit, Ahriman or Ahura Mainyu, king of darkness. Each king commanded an army, locked in constant battle. Each king had his special chiefs, archdemons for Ahriman and archangels for Ormazd. The archdemons were the spirits of evil things like destruction and anger; the archangels the spirits of good things like devotion and divine wisdom.

One of Ahriman's demons, the demon of anger, was named Aeshma and passed into Jewish lore as Ashmadai and into Christian lore as Asmodeus (more of him later). Other, lesser demons were Mitox, demon of lies, and Akatasa, demon of not-minding-one's-own-business. One female demon, the Nasu, was usually in the shape of a fly—which may have been an honor, since some stories say Ahriman was born as a fly. The Nasu was a demon of filth and decay who fed on dead creatures. When someone died, a ceremony called Sag-did was held to summon Ormazd's dogs and birds. When they came, they chased the Nasu away. If the ceremony was not performed, the Nasu could only be cast out by a complicated ritual involving a great deal of washing: the Nasu was chased from one part of the body to another by holy water until there was no unwashed place left for her.

According to Zoroastrianism, Ormazd and Ahriman both sprang from the same source, an exalted spirit known as "Boundless Time." Both started out being good, but Ahriman was jealous because Ormazd had been born first and was therefore just a little older. Ahriman was banished for his jealousy and, while Ormazd created all things that are good, his brother countered by doing the exact opposite—by creating evil and trying constantly to destroy the good. Like the Judeo-Christian God, Ormazd created man; and like Satan, Ahriman corrupted him. The battle between the brothers— between good and its opposite, evil—would continue, said Zoroaster, until a day of judgment when (again, as Christianity taught later) good would finally triumph.

The Gnostics, a religious sect which appeared sometime around the second century A.D., combined some aspects of Persian dualism with ideas from other philosophies and religions, including Christianity. Some Gnostics taught that it was the Devil or a Devil-like spirit who had created the world of humankind. Other sects extended this belief, saying that spiritual things, like the soul, were the work of God and therefore good, and physical things, like the body, were the work of the Devil and therefore bad. Along with these ideas came the one that shocked Christians the most: the idea that the forces of evil were equal to the forces of good. Christianity, although influenced by dualistic ideas, still taught that the Devil's power was inferior to God's. Any attempt to make them equal was, in the eyes of the Church, in itself evil. It was not long before Christians said that members of sects which taught that God and the Devil were equal must worship the Devil as much as they worshiped God, or even more. And, as Christianity grew in power, many members of such sects were burned at the stake as witches and heretics.

A heretic, basically, is anyone who does not follow the established religion. You'll remember that we said earlier that the gods of one religion were usually considered demons by any rival religion. The same kind of thinking was applied to heresy. The early Christians were considered heretics by established religions in Rome. But when Christians became more influential than members of other religions they turned around and called non-Christians heretics.

Another idea the early Christians added to what they borrowed from Persian dualism was the idea that evil, and therefore the Devil, could exist only with God's permission. Why should God allow evil? One reason given is that, without evil, people would not know what good is. The Devil, some Church authorities said, exists to give people a choice between good and evil; God gives people a chance to be good by allowing the Devil to tempt them.

But the Judeo-Christian Devil—Satan—was not always evil. There are many versions of how and why and even when he became so. In the play *Man and Superman*, by British writer George Bernard Shaw, the Devil says that most people think "the whole of this silly story is in the Bible"—but actually very little of it is.

The story of how Satan became evil originates primarily in what are known as the Apocrypha—books of Scriptures which are not officially accepted as part of the Bible. According to a story in the first book of Enoch, written in the second century B.C., evil came into the world when the "sons of Elohim" (God) looked down to earth from heaven, saw that the "daughters of men" were beautiful and left their heavenly post to go down to earth to them. Satan was among those sons of God. Like his brothers, he was not evil until he went to earth. He was simply an angel whose job was something like a lawyer's. When a problem was brought for judgment before the heavenly throne, Satan was the one who presented the opposing view. In fact, the original meaning of the word *satan* was probably just "adversary" or "opponent," words which do not stand for anything necessarily evil.

But to get back to the story of the sons of Elohim, it's probably safe to say that these angels became evil—became demons—because they went to earth to be with mortal women. Their children became demons too, although there's some confusion about how.

Some versions of the story say that their children, the giant Repha-im you read about in the last chapter, were born demons. Others say their children's ghosts became demons. And some versions say that, yes, some of their children were demons, but others were good, a whole group of superpeople called the Gibborim, who grew up to be heroes and who gave humankind art, military knowledge, and magic.

One of the important differences between this story about the beginning of evil and of Satan and other stories about the same thing is that it takes place *after* the creation of human beings. It is true that some early Christian authorities borrowed directly from Enoch and said that the reason the angels left heaven was to be with the daughters of men. But according to the prevailing Christian myth, the angels left heaven long before there were any daughters of men at all, or even any men and women to have daughters. Another difference is that, in Enoch, Satan was not singled out as the leader of the sons of Elóhim; he was just one of the boys, so to speak. But in later versions of the story, he was definitely their leader.

The usual reason given for Satan's "fall" from heaven is that Satan got a little too big for his britches and decided that he was as good as God; God, as a result, ordered him out (on August 1, some versions of the story point out carefully). With Satan went a lot of other angels who shared his views. No one seems to know exactly how many left, although some say it was a tenth of all the angels in heaven.

Before the fall Satan was the best, the smartest, the holiest, and the most beautiful of all the angels. Angels were divided into ranks or orders: seraphim, cherubim, thrones, dominions, virtues, powers, principalities, archangels, and angels. Some experts say that Satan started out as a cherub (if you've ever seen those fat little smiling babies people call cherubs, you'll see that he must have undergone quite a transformation after he fell from heaven!). Others say he was originally an angel or an archangel. Gregory the Great, pope from 590 to 604, had still another idea. He said Satan was a member of a special and rather unusual order called ophanim. When he fell, he took everyone else in the order with him. That must have been quite a sight, for, according to Gregory, the members of that order were flaming wheels with eyes all over them!

There are several versions of how Satan's fall actually happened. According to the Talmud, the books of Jewish law, it took place just after the creation of Adam—again, before there were any daughters of men. When God made Adam, the Talmud says, he asked all the angels to acknowledge how wonderful Adam was, and to say that he was king of the earth. Everyone agreed—except Satan, who said that since he thought he was as good as Adam or better, he didn't see why he should bow down to him. He also said that if God didn't like his attitude, he would place his own throne higher than God's to prove that he was not only better than Adam but also better than God himself. God, in his wrath at Satan's insubordination, threw him out of heaven along with all his friends.

An early Christian version of this story says that the rebellion in heaven was a reaction of the angels to God's *plan* to create Adam, not to the actual creation itself. They were upset because they felt that Adam, being made in God's image, would be happier than they, who were not. (One can see their point, if they looked anything like the ophanim!) Later Christian versions of the story say that Satan was expelled from heaven for challenging God's power in an overall sense, and that Adam was created to fill the gap left when Satan was expelled—some say to take his place in the "heavenly choir."

As you can see, the stories differ as to the way in which Satan challenged God, but most of them agree that pride was at the root of the challenge. The medieval Italian poet Dante said that Satan actually plotted to take over God's throne. Other writers said that he just tried to sit on it—a sort of symbolic taking-over. And still others said that all Satan did was refuse to worship God.

The *Malleus Maleficarum (Hammer of Witches)*, written in the fifteenth century as a handbook for judges who were trying people accused of being witches, gives still another form to Satan's pride and hence to his rebellion. According to the *Malleus*, he didn't want to make himself God's equal, but he did want to be put in charge of all the world's creatures—especially humankind. He was willing to acknowledge God's superiority so long as humanity was dependent on him rather than God for the good things of life. By the time the *Malleus* was written, the Church was teaching that the Devil was "Prince of This World" and that earthly pleasures were evil—so it would seem that, according to the *Malleus* anyway, Satan's rebellion was a rousing success!

Most authorities, however, termed it a dismal failure. Even in *Paradise Lost*, a long poem by the seventeenth-century poet John Milton (and perhaps the most famous account of Satan's fall in English), Satan ends up subdued, although for most of Milton's story he is a strong and sympathetic character.

Milton agrees that Satan's sin was pride and says Satan wanted "to set himself in glory above his peers." According to Milton, God created his Son while Satan was still in heaven, and before he created Adam. He then asked all the angels to bow down to his Son and said that he would cast out of heaven anyone who disobeyed. Satan angrily refused to bow, just as in the Talmudic version he refused to bow to Adam.

That night, Satan began plotting a rebellion. He was by no means alone in his fury, for about a third of the angels in heaven agreed to rebel with him. His plan was to build his own throne, equal to God's, in the northern part of heaven. When the plan was discovered, there was a great battle. Satan and his forces—who included Moloch and other pagan gods—put up a stiff fight, but in the end the archangels Michael and Gabriel, and finally God's Son, overcame them and drove them out of heaven.

They actually did fall when they were driven out, through miles and miles of empty space, and it took them quite a while to recover

when they landed. But even after his defeat and the terrifying fall through space, Satan was still determined to defy God. After a long discussion, he and his lieutenant Beelzebub decided to oppose God by doing evil, since they knew God hated evil. It would be, said Satan, "better to reign in hell than serve in heaven."

By this time, rumors of the creation of Adam had reached the fallen angels. Satan, thinking this might present a good opportunity for evildoing, made up his mind to see this new creature. After a long trip, he arrived in the Garden of Eden where, in the shape of a serpent, he flattered Adam's wife, Eve, into talking with him. Eve, amazed that a serpent could engage her in conversation, asked him where he had learned to talk. This question fit right into Satan's plan. Gleefully, he told her he had learned by eating the fruit of a certain tree, the Tree of Knowledge, from which, God had said, Adam and Eve must not eat on pain of death. But Satan cleverly talked Eve into tasting the fruit. Then Adam, out of love for her and a desire to share her fate, ate some too. Soon afterward, Sin and Death, allegorical characters who had formerly been stationed at the gates of hell, decided that Satan had been so successful they too could now enter the world to plague humankind.

Satan, of course, was delighted at his accomplishment. Now that God's creation, once so perfect, had been corrupted, God himself would kill it—or so Satan thought. Happily, he went home to hell, bragging of his success—but, to revise an old expression, pride goeth again before a fall. At the end of the story Satan and all his followers were turned into serpents and God postponed Adam's and Eve's death sentences by turning them out of Eden and letting them live for a long time in exile. Eve, God ruled, would have to "bring forth children in sorrow" and always obey her husband; Adam

Michael and other angels throwing Satan and his followers out of heaven. An illustration by Albrecht Dürer.

would have to eat the fruit of the Tree of Knowledge all his life (which probably was another way of saying that knowledge can make people sad). Both of them would have to die someday, but their children, God promised, would conquer Satan in the end and rise to sit at God's right hand.

In medieval mystery plays, which often reenacted the story of the fall, the whole tale is much simpler than in *Paradise Lost*. Satan, in those plays, started out sitting in a seat next to God. Then God left, telling everyone not to touch his throne. As soon as his back was turned, Satan not only touched his throne but also sat on it. The archangel Michael single-handedly drove him out of heaven. A French legend says this one-to-one battle between the Devil and Michael took place at Mont-Saint-Michel, a rocky island off the French coast.

In Russia, the idea that Satan decided to get revenge on God through Adam turns up in a still different legend. After God had shaped Adam's body out of clay, he left it for a minute in the care of his watchdog. But the dog's attention lapsed for a moment. Satan, who had been waiting for just such an opportunity, quickly made Adam susceptible to seventy different diseases—rather as a disease demon from the Fertile Crescent might have done.

Satan, for all his importance in many parts of the world, is by no means the only "devil chief" humankind has devised. Old Norse legend told of Loki, a mischief-making god, murderer of the beautiful god Balder. Loki, under the influence of Christianity, became almost Satan-like. One of the most interesting devil chiefs was the Jewish devil Samaël. Gregory the Great said that Samaël was a seraph who followed Satan out of heaven, but Hebrew tradition said that he was the leader of the rebel angels and, like Satan in the Christian tradition, became the head devil in hell. Samaël was also sometimes called an angel of death or a storm demon. Like Satan, he was usually pictured as being bright red in color. But the thing that made him really unique was that he was the husband of Lilith, who, in some legends, was Adam's first wife.

Lilith as a cat

Lilith was probably derived from our old friend the Lamme and from that whole crew of bloodthirsty female demons. But her story reads like a modern feminist saga. Adam and Lilith, it seems, had a terrific argument about which of them should be the boss, and Lilith refused to give in and say, "You should, dear, of course." Adam didn't understand that at all, so the argument went on until Lilith finally left him. She absolutely refused to go back, too, even though three angels tried to talk her into it. Lilith was punished cruelly for going against her husband's wishes: her children were killed. And so, like Lamia, the bereft Libyan queen, Lilith took her revenge by killing other women's children.

Samaël, says one legend, found Lilith when she was terribly lonely and mourning the loss of her children. He married her, and they had many children together, all of them demons. Some of them were succubi, female demons who taunt and tempt men at night, and others were among the most famous of Satan's troops in hell.

Another very important devil chief, and one very similar to Satan, was Iblis, head devil of the Arab world. A picture in a Persian manuscript shows him as being red, with the mane of a dragon, a protruding tongue, and prominent teeth. Devils who look like fish swim near him in a fiery lake, gulping down the souls of the damned.

The Koran, sacred book of Islam, describes the story of Iblis' fall from heaven very much the way the Talmud describes Satan's fall. Iblis and his followers, according to the Koran, were thrown out of heaven for saying they wouldn't worship Adam. "Adam is only made out of clay," complained Iblis, who was a high-ranking angel. "I was made of fire and am therefore better than he."

After his fall, Iblis went to Eden to tempt Eve. In one story, the only way he could get in was by smuggling himself there in the mouth of a serpent. He talked to Eve from the serpent's mouth— which is why everyone thinks he actually turned into a talking serpent!

After the Tree of Knowledge episode, Allah (God) sentenced Iblis to hell, but Iblis begged so hard not to be sent there that Allah gave him power over sinners on earth. Until judgment day, says one story, Iblis would be allowed to live in this world, but only in "unclean" places—like tombs. He was also condemned to eat only those foods forbidden to Moslems and to drink only alcoholic beverages. He would be allowed to father seven devils for every human born—but despite their numbers, Iblis and his followers would never be able to prevail against people who were true to their religion.

In that, too, Iblis was not unlike Satan.

3
Who the Devil?

LATE ONE NIGHT when Martin Luther, the sixteenth-century German Protestant leader, was sitting in his room translating the Bible, he suddenly looked up—and saw the Devil. The fiend insisted on reading what Luther had written and soon Luther found himself in the midst of a furious argument about the technicalities of a biblical passage. The good Luther, who had been without food for days and was tired and sick, finally lost his temper, picked up his full inkstand, and hurled it with all his strength at Satan. Instantly, the Devil disappeared, and the ink hit the wall, making a dark stain.

Some versions of this story don't say what the Devil looked like. Others say only that he was ugly. One, written a couple of generations after Luther's death, described the Devil as a monk. Luther recognized him, says this version, when he noticed that the "monk's" hands had claws instead of fingers!

It's not surprising that no one seems to agree on just what Luther's Devil looked like for, according to most beliefs, the Devil can take on any shape he wishes. He can be male or female, animal or human, visible or invisible. He can change his size if he wants and he can even become a nonliving thing, like fog or water. Beware the Devil, people have cautioned one another down through the ages, for he is a creature of many disguises and you never can be sure just how or when he is going to appear.

Be especially careful, warn the old wives' tales, when you are in bad trouble. Be wary of a handsome stranger or an ugly beast if

Martin Luther getting the best of the Devil.

either offers help. The Devil is always willing to help people in need —in exchange for their immortal souls. He is so willing, say the superstitious, that you should never call out his name; say "the deuce" or "the dickens" instead, for the Devil will always come—in one shape or another—when called. Even Noah, according to the following Moslem story, got into trouble by carelessly using the Devil's name (although it was a put-up job).

It had rained, as nearly everyone knows, for forty days and nights, and Noah was busy loading his Ark with a male and a female of every species. Most creatures were nervous if not downright terrified, but not even the rising floodwaters could distract the Devil from his desire to do evil. He wanted to get aboard the Ark so he could go on working after the flood to fill the world with sin and grief. Cleverly, he grabbed hold of the donkey's tail and pulled it so hard the poor beast couldn't move. Noah impatiently yelled at the donkey, "Come on, you devil, hurry up!"—innocently giving the Devil the invitation he needed to board the Ark. Once he was there, says another version of the story, he lost no time in boring a hole in the Ark in order to sink it and drown all its passengers. But a brave hedgehog stuffed itself into the hole, thus saving the human race and all the animals.

Despite the Devil's ability to shape-shift, most people have always thought that he has one basic shape. That shape, though, has changed over the centuries, depending on people's religion, background, and view of life in general. If you called on the Devil in early Christian times, for example, it was likely that he'd appear to you looking a lot like the Greek god Pan, complete with horns, hooves, and a tail—or like Pazuzu, with wings.

Gradually, however, the Devil's basic shape became less like an ancient god's or demon's and more like a human being's. At first his human shape was usually ugly. The Devil was considered "God's ape," the mimic of God but his exact opposite in every way. Because God was beautiful, the Devil had to be ugly.

Later, though, when people began thinking of the Church as severely strict and of the Devil as a symbol of freedom and pleasure, Satan became less ugly. At times when ordinary people rebelled against the Church and the rich ruling classes who controlled it, Satan, who of course was himself a rebel, was downright handsome. And today, when many people consider religion a somewhat remote philosophical structure instead of a total way of life, the Devil is often thought of as a shapeless spirit—an abstract force opposite to God's.

It was perhaps the fifteenth- and sixteenth-century trials held by the Inquisition (a Catholic body formed to try people accused of heresy and witchcraft) that gave us the most varied descriptions of the Devil. Here are some of the shapes—basic or otherwise—in which the Devil supposedly appeared to people who were accused of associating with him:

- a red-faced man
- a pale man
- a white man
- a black man
- a tall man
- a short man
- an old man
- a young man
- a boy
- a hairy man
- a beautiful man; perfection
- a man with horns
- a crippled man
- a strong man
- a pig
- a rooster
- a crow
- a fly
- a goat
- a wolf

All those shapes are pretty straightforward, though, and not particularly scary. Here, at the risk of offending the Devil (who is said to be on the vain side and unhappy about all the unflattering ways people describe him) are some other ways he is described:
- The Devil smells bad—like the sulphurous brimstone of hell.
- He is cold; his touch is icy.
- His tongue is thick and ugly, his neck long, his hands like claws.

• His nose is over a foot long. The reason: in the tenth century, St. Dunstan pulled it with fire tongs, and it has never been the same since!

• He breathes fire.

• He has donkey's ears.

• He is covered all over with feathers; he also has horns, a big mouth, a tail, hooves, a red beard, and the long nose he got from St. Dunstan.

• He has three faces.

• He has red eyes; or he has huge black eyes; or he is covered all over with eyes; or he has no eyes at all!

• He has a claw on his right foot, and his left foot is a hoof.

• He is as hairy as a pagan woods god.

• He is huge. According to Dante, he is what amounts to one and a third miles tall! He also has three heads, one black, one red, and the last yellowish. Each head has a set of wings.

• He is very thin and clothed in armor; he has no joints in his arms and legs.

• He has the face of an ancient Assyrian demon.

• His nose is like "the beak of an eagle" and he has "great burning eyes," according to testimony at the witchcraft trial of John Fian in Scotland in 1590. His legs are hairy and his feet are like a griffin's; he has claws on his hands. (Griffins were mythical animals with the hind legs and back paws of lions.)

• He is eight feet tall, said Collin de Plancy, a nineteenth-century writer who claimed to have seen him. He has a tail, only because so many people insisted he had one that one sprouted. His horns grew to please nursemaids who wanted to scare children with terrible descriptions of the Devil.

One reason, perhaps, for the bizarre nature of some of these descriptions is that most people believed that whatever shape he took, the Devil could never achieve a perfect imitation of any

A sixteenth-century artist's view of the Devil.

A nineteenth-century artist's view of the Devil.

creature created by God. Therefore, there always had to be some flaw in him or in any shape he shifted to. In one thirteenth-century story, the Devil himself spoke of this, rather sadly, confiding that in human shape he and his followers "have no bottoms."

Another flaw the Devil is frequently said to have is a limp, because he hurt his leg when he fell from heaven, or because he was hurt in the battle. One story says that St. Michael the archangel cornered him in a castle on Mont-Saint-Michel. The Devil managed to escape to the roof but then found there was only one way to go farther—to jump. He went ahead and jumped, but broke his leg when he landed, and it never healed properly.

In African countries the Devil usually has white skin, but in European ones he is usually black. Have you ever heard the term "printer's devil"? Today it usually means a printer's errand boy or apprentice, but one explanation for its origin is that Aldus Manutius, a fifteenth-century Venetian printer, had a black slave as an assistant. Instead of realizing he was black, some people thought he was an imp from hell! Racial prejudice no doubt has something to do with the fact that whites have often said the Devil is black. But there's another reason too, and it is perhaps as strong. Black is the color most often connected with death and the terrors of night— which have always been closely associated with the Devil.

Red, like the fiery furnaces of hell, has also always been a popular devil color, especially in Oriental countries. Even when the Devil is not red all over, he is often pictured with a red beard and red hair. The old Egyptian wind demon, Typhon, had a red beard, as did Judas Iscariot, who betrayed Christ. In Spain, however, the Devil was sometimes said to be green, a color thought holy by the Moors, who conquered Spain in the eighth century. As you can see, most people picked a color for the Devil which meant something evil to them.

Black clothes were usually the Devil's favorite, and red his next favorite, but he also occasionally wore green, gray, or yellow. The style of his clothes was usually the style of the period he appeared in. The Devil dressed very well most of the time and often showed a great weakness for hats. His collection seems to have ranged from simple woolen caps to the most elaborate of French creations with long gracefully waving plumes.

The Devil has worn almost as many names as he has worn disguises, often adopting local names as he adopted local dress. He has also taken the names of his chief demons, especially Beelzebub and Asmodeus. Sometimes he is called Mephistopheles and sometimes Lucifer. Often his homelier nicknames are complicated names made simple, perhaps because people couldn't pronounce the original ones. The devil name Bellephon, for example, eventually became Billy Ruffian! Some of Satan's other nicknames are:

- The Baker (because he "bakes" souls in hell)
- The Black Bogey
- Old Horny
- Old Harry
- Old Hairy
- Old Scratch
- Old Nick

This last one, Old Nick, is an especially common devil name, although no one is sure of its origin. One theory is that it comes from the name of Neptune, ancient Roman sea god whom sailors feared as much as they admired; Neptune caused storms and therefore seemed diabolical. Another theory is that Old Nick comes from the name of a Saxon god, Nicor—again, a sea and water god who caused storms and drownings. According to still another theory, Old Nick is simply short for Old Iniquity (*iniquity* means "wickedness"). But most experts say Old Nick comes from St. Nicholas, the good bishop of Myra who gave presents to children and eventually became Santa Claus. Why make a devil out of the wonderful S. Claus? Because, in Puritan times, poor Santa was considered frivolous and even evil. Christmas, if it was observed at all, was a time for solemnity, not a time for merriment as was the pagan feast of Yule, which came at the same time of year.

In pictures, Satan was sometimes shown carrying a pitchfork or trident—a three-pronged fork like the one that Neptune was supposed to have held in his hand. Some scholars say the trident symbolized the power the Devil had over the earth, the air, and the sea. Others say it was an ancient fertility symbol. The Devil has also appeared armed with a spear or a thunderbolt or a hammer, and sometimes he has carried a basket for taking souls to hell. But he was more likely to be shown with a skin bag for that purpose. The souls, it seems, kept finding ways to escape through the mesh of the basket!

It's hard to say which of the shapes the Devil has appeared in, regardless of his costumes, have been his own and which have been assumed, but it's certainly safe to say there seem to have been no limits to his ingenuity. In order to fool people and to get himself into the most advantageous position for doing evil, the Devil could turn himself into an angel or even, according to some sources, assume the shape of Christ. He could combine shapes, too, and could appear, as did many of his demons, as a horrible monster made up of parts of different animals—a beast with a camel's head, for example, with snakes for hair and a lion's teeth, plus horns, wings, claws, hooves, and a dragon's tail. Many of the animal shapes assumed by the Devil have been reminiscent of the shapes of ancient pagan gods. The most obvious of these, of course, was the goatlike shape of Pan. Other animal shapes used by the Devil were those of animals sacred to non-Christian religions. The Devil sometimes appeared as a bull or a cat, for example; both were sacred to Egyptian cults.

Sometimes it suited the Devil's purpose to take on the shape of a woman, especially when he was trying to convince a man to sell his soul or do evil. A young Scottish man in the seventeenth century was actually tried in court for being the servant of a woman who everyone thought was the Devil in disguise.

"Well," you may be saying, "who the devil [careful!] can tell who the Devil really is and what he looks like if he slips shapes on and off as easily as we change clothes?" The Russian writer Nikolai Gogol had the answer. According to a story he wrote, if you want to see the Devil's true shape, you must wait till St. John's Eve (June 21). Find yourself a mustard seed and keep it near you on that night. At midnight, the Devil will appear in his true shape.

What he'll do then, of course, is another matter entirely!

4
What the Devil?

ONE OF THE REASONS why it's hard to be sure what the Devil would do if he really could appear in his true shape on St. John's Eve is that his personality varies as much as his shapes and his costumes. Dante, in his poem *The Inferno*, described Satan as being utterly defeated. He might have been strong and powerful once, but by the time of the visit to hell Dante describes in the poem, there was nothing left of the Great Adversary's former strength. All he could do was weep and grind his jaws like a cow chewing her cud, while weakly folding and unfolding his wings around his three heads.

Not so the later Satan of Milton in *Paradise Lost*. He was almost glorious by contrast. Milton's Satan, though defeated in the end, was proudly defiant, and his evil powers were conquerable only after a tremendous struggle. There is no question that he was once the most beautiful and intelligent angel in heaven. The only reason Milton's Satan isn't quite a great hero is that he is evil. But even so, he seems almost as noble as a fallen king and, in his sorrow and anger, as worthy of understanding.

These are, of course, two extreme views of the Devil's personality. There have been many others, some of them, like early ideas about his physical appearance, combining various characteristics of pagan gods and ancient demons. For example, in some stories the Devil had an enormous appetite, like an ancient hunger demon. Superstitious bakers in Germany used to mix up more biscuit dough than they needed to fill their regular orders so they could make a

few biscuits for the Devil first. That way, they could be sure he wouldn't burn the main batch of biscuits out of anger at not having his hunger satisfied.

A devil who burns biscuits is not nearly so terrifying as a devil who causes death and destruction. Some legends say that the Devil has caused disease ever since that time during the creation when he made Adam susceptible to illness. As to death—well, the Devil's main job has always been to get souls for hell. To do that, he often had to kill his victims. Beforehand he usually made a deal, a formal contract called a pact, with the person whose soul he wanted. He would promise to give the person anything he or she wanted for a certain period of time, at the end of which he would be free to take the person's soul. That usually meant he killed his victim or in some way caused his victim's death.

People usually made pacts with the Devil when they were so desperate for money that they would promise anything to get it. Usually all the Devil had to do was be in the right place at the right time and appear to people when they were especially unhappy or greedy. Nonetheless, because he "fished" for souls, the Devil was sometimes pictured as a fisherman—the opposite of the Apostle Peter, who was a "fisher of men" engaged in finding souls for heaven.

As pact maker or fisher of souls, disease-bringer, or whatever, the Devil has gone through many personality changes depending on place and time. In northern Europe, for example, the Devil was usually tough and terrifying, as were many of the gods in that part of the world, and as was the climate. In southern Europe, however, the Devil was more apt to be sensual and pleasure-loving; the gods there were more happy-go-lucky and the climate was gentler.

During the twelfth and thirteenth centuries, when people tended

The Devil disciplining the damned. An illustration by John Baptist Medina for Milton's Paradise Lost.

to think of God and the saints in human terms, they thought of the Devil that way too. In fact, it was easier to think of the Devil that way than God or the saints. You could feel closer to Satan, because he did have faults, than you could to God, who had none.

During the Inquisition's witch-hunts, however, when the Church in its fervor found witches and devils under every bush, the Devil was taken seriously again as a creature to be feared. He was a very real physical being of great power and cunning, a double-crosser, and unquestionably evil. But when the witch furor had died down and people began viewing the Devil as a symbol of freedom and independence, they gave him a less evil personality and a handsome physical appearance. Today, when the Devil is thought of as flesh and blood instead of as a disembodied spirit, he's frequently seen in the same way.

The Devil was always believed to be a good actor, no matter what part of the world he was in or what era. There was many a time he played a part in order to be able to go places or do things he couldn't have done if he had shown his true shape. Thus, he often played the part of a monk, priest, or other clergyman, as he did when he appeared to Luther. He even preached sermons, sometimes taking over for a clergyman who couldn't make it to a service! The Devil has also played the part of a scholar, a soldier, an athlete —and, as one might expect given his early role in heaven as the Adversary, he has always been very good at pretending to be a lawyer, as this folk story shows:

A poor soldier once foolishly trusted an innkeeper to guard his money. But, "What money?" barked the innkeeper when the soldier asked for it back. "You gave me no money." And he slammed the door in the soldier's face.

The soldier beat fiercely at the door until he smashed it down. Unfortunately someone saw him and he landed in jail, charged with attempted burglary. In despair he lay in his cell; death, he knew, could easily be the penalty for such an offense. Perhaps a good lawyer could help him. But no lawyer would take his case.

By the day of his trial, the soldier was convinced that nothing could save him. Then just as court was called to order, a young man dressed in a feathered hat stepped up to the judge and said, "Your Honor, I will defend this man." The soldier held his breath; it seemed too good to be true. Surely the judge would not let a stranger speak on his behalf. But the judge had no objection.

The elegantly dressed young lawyer calmly but eloquently explained the facts of the case to the court. The soldier felt a spurt of hope. He had never seen this lawyer before, but the man was telling the story truthfully, exactly as he would have told it himself, even to the slamming of the door.

Meanwhile the innkeeper, growing paler with every word the lawyer said, was getting fidgety. Finally he could contain himself no longer. "Devil take me if I have the money!" he shouted.

That was all the Devil—for of course the lawyer was none other than Satan—needed. Spreading his wings, he grabbed the evil innkeeper and rose with him up, up, straight through the roof. The innkeeper's wife, without a moment's hesitation, returned the stolen money. The soldier, of course, was delighted—but then so was the Devil, for he had cleverly snared another soul for hell.

The role of lawyer was a good one for the Devil for another reason besides the fact that lawyering had perhaps been his original job in heaven. As the Church encouraged people to docilely obey its rules and accept its teachings, the Devil was increasingly accused of encouraging those people who dared to ask questions. God stood for faith, the Devil for independent thinking and reason. The Devil on earth was as much a rebel against the establishment as he had been in heaven.

Whenever science was suspect, the Devil was a scientist. In medieval times, the Church accused scientists of working against the will of God, largely because scientists question things rather than accepting them on faith. That meant that science was a tool of the Devil—black magic, even. Any scientist whose lab smelled of sulphur was in double trouble, for visitors who got a whiff of the pungent stuff would be sure the Devil had just left or perhaps was still there, lurking behind the scientist's suspicious-looking jars and tubes and pots.

Science and invention go hand and hand, so it should come as no surprise that the Devil was supposed to be a brilliant inventor. Even in modern times people have said that new things—cars, planes, television—are diabolical, although often they've only been kidding or speaking figuratively. In 1828 an Ohio school board said that the railroad was "a device of the Devil," and as recently as 1972 a judge in county Kildare, Ireland, ruled that psychedelic lights were "designed by the Devil" since they could, according to him, drive people crazy.

The Devil has also been credited with nonscientific inventions like money and playing cards and other instruments of gambling. (Cards have been called "The Devil's Bible," and dice, "the Devil's Bones.") The Devil loved gambling himself and played for very high stakes, as you can see from this story:

Glamis Castle in Scotland is best known as the place where Shakespeare's hero Macbeth committed murder, but it has some other claims to fame also. The most gruesome story about Glamis Castle, which takes place in the fifteenth century, centers on one Earl Patie, who had, to put it mildly, a bad reputation among his neighbors. This lord of the castle was an inveterate gambler, so dedicated to his cards that he played even on Sundays, something no right-thinking or God-fearing person in those days would have dreamed of doing. To play cards, of course (unless you're given to solitaire, which the earl was not), you need a partner. But partners were hard to come by on Sundays.

One cold and stormy Sunday night, Earl Patie was so desperate that he asked, then ordered his servants to play with him—but none of them would. They were good people and would not break the Sabbath.

"Very well," growled the earl, stomping off furiously to his gaming room, "I'll play with the Devil if need be."

As you'll remember, the Devil usually comes when he's called and he isn't any too particular about the nature of the summons when there's a possibility of nabbing another soul. Sure enough, as soon as the earl had spoken, a tall figure, heavily wrapped in a thick cloak, entered the gaming room. While the earl stared, the stranger sat down, saying that he would play if the earl would give him, if he won, anything he asked for.

"Of course," said the earl, the prospect of a game snapping him out of his fright. "Of course, anything. I am a rich man. Only let us begin the game!"

But the stranger made him sign something first, before they played.

From that point on the story gets cloudy, perhaps because the Devil wanted it that way. No one seems to know exactly how the game progressed, or even what game it was. But the score must have been close, for the sound of swearing boomed so loudly through the castle that the earl's frightened servants ran to the door and listened. The butler stooped to look through the keyhole, and *whap!* There was a yell from the stranger inside the room and at the same time bright hot flames shot through the keyhole, straight at the prying butler. The butler survived, it seems, but the mysterious stranger disappeared and for five years nothing more was heard or seen of him.

At the end of five years' time the earl died. It was whispered that the stranger—the Devil—had taken his soul. And that rumor was hard to dispute, for every Sunday night from then on in that very same room in Glamis Castle, the two played their game again—and again and again—as if Earl Patie, still the gambler, was desperately trying to win back the soul he'd sold so long before.

In addition to gambling, the Devil loved all other pleasures and entertainments, light or heavy, popular or refined. All the arts were his special province, Church authorities said in the days when the arts were considered frivolous and dangerous threats to propriety and faith. The Devil helped artists in the same way he helped clergymen, finishing their work for them when they couldn't; he even worked on some of the carvings that decorate churches. He's been accused of dictating the world's most controversial books to their unsuspecting authors, and he has a reputation for stealing the manuscripts of books which are unflattering to him. (He doesn't seem to have minded this one, although a few pages were missing for a while!)

The Devil was also thought to be a fine engineer, especially good at building bridges. Perhaps this was because bridge building was so difficult and dangerous before the days of modern construction equipment that it seemed to require a superhuman effort. In most stories about the Devil as bridge builder, the Devil says he will help build a bridge if he can have as payment the first one—or two or three—who cross it. But it is rare that he collects.

The apprentice architect of a certain bridge across the Danube River in Europe bet his master that he would finish his bridge before his master finished a cathedral he was working on. The master accepted the bet.

The poor apprentice slaved night and day on his bridge but made little progress. "I wish," he sighed one day when everything had toppled again, "that it were the Devil and not I who was building this old bridge!"

No sooner were the words out of his mouth than a holy-looking friar appeared and said, "I will build your bridge, apprentice, if you give me the first three who cross it."

The apprentice may not have been the best bridge builder in the world, but he was smart enough to know the Devil when he saw him. He was also smart enough not to let on he knew. "Would you really?" he asked innocently. "Oh, thank you . . . father!" And he smiled politely and settled back to watch while the Devil worked.

By the time the fiend was close to finished, the apprentice had thought of a plan. Off he went to round up the three to cross first. Before long he came back with them, and at the moment when the Devil stepped back to view his work, the apprentice stepped into the road—and drove a rooster, a hen, and a dog across the bridge in front of him!

Some of the Devil's works, as you can see, turned into good deeds, even if his purpose was always to get more souls for hell. He has often done good things for the downtrodden, acting sometimes as a sort of Robin Hood figure and helping the poor get money from the rich. Sometimes, for example, he took revenge on innkeepers who watered down their beer and on shopkeepers who instead of

Demons punishing women who sold bad ale.

giving people a pound of what they wanted gave them only fifteen ounces.

Despite the Devil's many talents, however, he had only limited powers. God permitted him to tempt Christ, but according to religious teachings, only for two very special reasons. First, said the Church, it was God's way of showing Christ what terrible temptations human beings are subject to. And second, God hoped that Christ, by resisting Satan's temptation, would inspire human beings to do the same. The Devil was also allowed to tempt the biblical character Job—only in order to show Job's loyalty to God. The Devil has always ended up powerless, says the Church, against the forces of good.

That doesn't mean, though, that the Devil wasn't sometimes capable of outwitting others. There's many a story in which the Devil gives a person gold—and the gold, not long afterward, turns into something dreadful, often toads or cats' claws. The Devil was well named "Father of Lies," for he was a dedicated double-crosser. He had a reputation for never breaking a contract which would benefit him—but when it came to bargains in which he did not stand to gain a soul for hell, he usually backed down. Once, when he hired a demon to build a barn for him, he made a rooster crow shortly before the job was done. That may seem like an insignificant trick—until you take into account that the Devil knew all evil creatures must fly away at dawn and that the demon, hearing the rooster crow, would therefore leave without collecting his pay.

Even though he occasionally disguised himself in woman's shape, the Devil had a reputation for disliking women. Women, however, perhaps because of what happened to Eve, were said to be easy marks for his charm. Many a woman, tortured by the Inquisition into "admitting" she was a witch, told how the Devil had seduced her. Sometimes the Devil's liaisons with women resulted in children. One of the most famous was the magician Merlin, an important character in the British King Arthur legends. Occasionally, a woman tried to reform the Devil through her love, or even put in a good word for him in heaven, but usually the Devil's affairs turned out badly for all concerned. Once in Portugal he was so fascinated by a woman named Lupa that he disguised himself as a woman and became her maid. But before Satan could reveal his true identity, Lupa died, with two saints guarding her closely from him and saving her soul.

In one Spanish story, the Devil actually succeeded in marrying a girl. But he was soon outwitted by a shrewd old woman who told the girl to beat him with a blessed olive branch on their wedding night. The old woman made sure their room was tightly locked and then she stationed herself outside, holding an empty bottle over the keyhole. The Devil, fleeing from the assault, soon found that the only escape route was through the keyhole—and of course he ended up in the old woman's bottle. It was years, according to the story, before he managed to escape.

The story doesn't say where the Devil went when he came out of the bottle, and it's hard to guess, for people have had differing opinions about his favorite haunts. You might find him in Paris, France, which used to be considered a "sinful" city by some people. He might show up in Scotland, where there are a number of places named after him, or even in the United States, maybe in Devils Lake, North Dakota; Devils Den, California; Devils Elbow, Missouri; Devils Slide, Utah; Devils Tower, Wyoming; or Devils Track, Minnesota—to name just a few possibilities.

In general, according to most legends, you'd do well to look for the Devil in the north instead of the south. In *Paradise Lost*, remember, he planned to build his rival throne in the north of heaven. The book of Job in the Bible places hell in the north, and in medieval plays, hell was in the northern part of the stage. And it is, of course, in hell, be it in the north or deep in the bowels of the earth, where the Devil makes his home—hell, where fire burns so hot it must find release in great volcanic eruptions and earthquakes;

where brimstone reeks and hot embers scorch damned souls; where imps laugh and the Devil is at home with his demons. Some say that he is in chains there, tied up for his sins until the Day of Judgment. But even if that is so, there is no shortage of evil in the world, for it is said that no one chained Satan's demons, and they are still free to walk the earth and do his bidding.

One artist's version of Satan's punishment.

5
All the Demons of Hell

PEOPLE USED TO ARGUE about how many angels could fit on the head of a pin. No one seems to have played that intellectual game with demons, but people have certainly disagreed about how many, small or large, lived in hell with Satan after his fall. In the sixteenth century, a German writer named Johannes Wierus made the whole question into a mathematical puzzle by painstakingly dividing hell's demons into 1,111 legions of 6,666 demons each. That comes out to a grand total of 7,405,926—considerably fewer than the estimate of Paracelsus, a doctor of roughly the same era, who simplified the matter by saying there were so many demons they filled the air. His idea was similar to that of a thirteenth-century abbot who had said the demons were as numerous as grains of sand.

In general, the demon count seems to get larger the further back you go in history. In the fifteenth century, for example, the theologian Alphonso de Spina calculated that there were 133,306,668 demons—a considerable drop from the figure of 1,758,064,176 which someone had come up with a couple of centuries earlier. There have been other estimates: 2,400 legions, said one (that comes to 15,998,400 demons, if a legion is 6,666, which it isn't always); 1,000 million, said another. But the figure usually accepted was Wierus' 7,405,926—except by those who believed that hell's forces were constantly increasing as evil souls died and became demons, as demons reproduced, and as additional angels disagreed with God and left heaven.

You'll remember that people thought the angels of heaven were divided into orders: seraphim, archangels, and so forth. Since hell was considered the exact opposite of heaven, demons were similarly divided and, as there were "patron saints" in heaven, there were also what amounted to "patron demons" in hell, usually guardians of various professions. Some demonologists (people who study demons) said the demons formed a vast army. Wierus, for example, said the pagan god Moloch was a demon general-in-chief and that the ex-god Baal (who, as you'll remember, was more or less the original of Moloch in that Moloch was a "version" of him) was his second in command. Another expert said that Moloch was commander of sixty-six legions. But Moloch has also been described as a king—a wise king ruling in the eastern part of hell, with a hoarse voice, three heads (one of a toad, one of a small man, and one of a cat), and the power to make people invisible. As you can see, there was no more agreement about the roles demons played in hell than there was about how many of them lived there in the first place. And, to make things even more confusing, some demonologists gave each demon a number of "jobs" in hell. Wierus, for example, called Moloch "Prince of the Land of Tears" as well as general-in-chief.

Surprising as it may seem, Satan was not always placed at the head of hell's hierarchy. Some Italian writers, continuing the tradition of ancient Rome, said that the god Pluto was king of hell. Wierus said that the demon Beelzebub, who, according to some people, was patron demon of governesses, had ruled hell since Christ's crucifixion. It seems that when Christ died, Satan wanted to claim his soul for hell; Beelzebub, however, was shocked by this idea. When Christ went down to hell to free the saints imprisoned there, he rewarded Beelzebub by putting him in charge and demoting Satan to Leader of the Opposition, which means he was more or less back to his original role of Adversary. It was something like being chief Republican when the Democrats are in power, or vice versa.

In *Paradise Lost,* however, these roles are reversed: Beelzebub is Satan's second in command. In other descriptions of hell, he is the power behind Satan's throne—and in still others, the real king of hell is Lucifer, and Pluto, Satan, and Beelzebub are governors. Ready for one more? Pluto has also been called "Prince of Fire" and his wife, Proserpina, "Princess of Mischievous Spirits," which makes her sound deceptively frivolous. She was also known as the arch-she-devil, however, which indicates she was actually a good deal more sinister and important. Here's another: Lucifer as emperor, Beelzebub as prince, and a demon named Astaroth as grand duke. Astaroth has also been named hell's ruler, along with Belphegor and Leviathan. The nineteenth-century author Sheridan le Fanu divided hell into ten kingdoms ruled by five kings: Lucifer, Beelzebub, Belial, Astaroth, and Phlegethon.

Confused?

Okay, let's backtrack for a minute and look at some of these demons more closely, starting with, say, Beelzebub.

Beelzebub's the one who has always been associated with flies, so he probably harks back to ancient Persia. He was also worshiped by the Canaanites as "Lord of the Flies," and no one's ever forgotten it. As late as the sixteenth century when a fly flew out of a possessed woman's mouth (possession is the phenomenon in which a demon supposedly enters a person's body and controls it) people said, in effect, "God be praised! She is free now. See how Beelzebub has just left her."

In hell, according to Wierus, Beelzebub founded an order of knighthood called the Order of the Fly. Many of the important demons were members. Any demon who did his or her job especially well could become eligible for the Grand Cross of the Order of the Fly—a sort of infernal Congressional Medal of Honor.

Beelzebub wasn't always in fly shape, though. He has also been

Beelzebub, Lord of the Flies.

described as tall, with horns, wings, and a lion's tail. That sounds pretty horrible, but according to a legend in Brittany, France, no one has anything to fear from Beelzebub anymore. He is dead, the legend says, killed by St. Michael and buried near—guess where? Right—Mont-Saint-Michel!

The demon Astaroth also goes way back to ancient times, but he went through more changes than Beelzebub in the shift from pagan god to infernal demon. Believe it or not, Astaroth probably started out female and had his origins in a group of goddesses, also called Astaroth, who were worshiped in Canaan along with the Baalim. He may also have been related to a Phoenician goddess called Astarte.

Astaroth, according to some demonologists, was very ugly and apparently needed a deodorant—that is, if anyone has ever invented an antibrimstone spray. He also had a reputation for being lazy, which makes it hard to believe that he was either ruler of hell or, as Wierus said, "a mighty lord" in command of forty legions— and Grand Treasurer to boot. Astaroth knew everything and could predict the future, Wierus said, but the most intriguing thing about him was that he claimed he had been forced out of heaven along with Satan and the rebels very much against his will.

Belial, who was one of Sheridan le Fanu's five demon kings, was, according to an old book of magic, one of the first and most beautiful angels to fall from heaven. He had a nice voice, perhaps left over from his days as an angel, and he was a good demon to know if you were a witch who needed a familiar—an imp, usually in animal shape, to work for you and make sure you did your job. Belial, it was thought, recommended only the best familiars. Belial was also good to know if you wanted a political favor or if you had a court case coming up. He was a skillful lawyer, although he lost his biggest case, one in which he claimed that it was illegal for Christ to have any control over the earth, the sea, or hell.

Belial, unlike many of his colleagues in hell, did not start out as a pagan god but instead sprang fron a misinterpretation of the He-brew word for "godlessness" in the Bible. According to some sources, people who read the word thought it was the name of a demonic being instead of the name of a quality. The idea persisted, and by the sixteenth century Belial the demon had become so important that some experts even claimed he was the ruler of hell. Others said he commanded as many as eighty legions.

Leviathan, the demon who, according to one description, shared the supreme throne of hell with Astaroth and Belphegor, was said by some demonologists to have been one of the children the ancient demons Lilith and Samaël produced after their marriage. He (or she; Leviathan sometimes appeared as female) was, according to Hebrew tradition, slated to kill, on the Day of Judgment, a monster-turned-demon named Behemoth. Behemoth, whose special job in hell was to serve wine, was rather stupid and had an enormous appetite. He looked like an elephant and, according to the Bible, "eateth grass as an ox, moveth his tail like a cedar, [and has] bones . . . like bars of iron." Leviathan was also a biblical creature and

Behemoth

was usually seen as the seagoing equivalent of Behemoth—in fact, some said Leviathan was the whale that swallowed Jonah. In demonology, Leviathan, who had hide so tough few spears could penetrate it, was hell's chief admiral and patron demon of ambassadors.

Yes, ambassadors. As a matter of fact, hell, according to Wierus, had a diplomatic corps. Belial, the honey-tongued lawyer, was ambassador to Turkey. The ambassador to England was Mammon, ancient god of greed, and Belphegor was ambassador to France. It's anybody's guess as to who Wierus would have chosen as emissary to the United States or Canada had he lived a couple of centuries later, but no doubt he would have thought of someone!

One of the best-known demons was seldom listed among the major rulers of hell, although he was sometimes called both prince and king of the demons. This was Asmodeus, another son of Lilith and Samaël. He was demon of lust, a dandy and patron of fashion, fastidious enough to hate bad smells, but also a gambler and "man of the world," not to mention a mathematician, engineer, astronomer, and sorcerer as well. He was also an excellent storyteller—at least legend has it that it was Asmodeus, not the Italian author Boccaccio, who wrote the stories in the famous fourteenth-century book *The Decameron*. In hell, Asmodeus ran the gambling houses, among other things.

But Asmodeus had another side too, an older, more primitive identity. When he was so inclined, he appeared not as a dandy at all but as a goat, or as a hideous man with wings, or even as a

Asmodeus

fire-breathing monster with the tail of a snake and three heads, one a human's, one a ram's, and one a bull's. When he appeared in any of those forms he was usually angry and carried a lance. He carried a lance back in ancient Persia too, where he was called Aeshma—remember?—and was, as spirit of anger, of impure fire, and of lust, one of Ahriman's followers.

The Hebrews called this same demon Aschmedai. For them, he was also an angry, lustful demon. The Apocryphal Book of Tobit says he was in love with a woman, Sarah, and was so jealous that he would not let any other man near her. Poor Sarah married seven different men, but Aschmedai killed each of them, one after the other, on their respective wedding nights. When Tobit proposed, God took pity on Sarah and sent his angel Raphael to help her. Raphael, cleverly remembering that Aschmedai hated bad smells, told Tobit to burn some fish liver and hearts on his wedding night. Sure enough, that made Aschmedai forget all about Sarah and flee far away into Egypt.

It was Asmodeus who tricked the mighty King Solomon, the one who supposedly built a temple to Moloch as well as the famous Jewish Temple. The latter temple was considered such an amazing construction feat that some people said Solomon could never have done it without demonic aid. Solomon, according to one of many stories about him, owned a magic ring, given him by the archangel Michael, with which he could control demons. He used this ring during the construction of the Temple to force Asmodeus and his friends to work for him as stonecutters. Naturally the demons weren't too pleased at being enslaved by Solomon, so Asmodeus laid plans to get the ring away from him. One version of this story says that Asmodeus taunted Solomon by saying, over and over, "I bet you'd be nothing if you didn't have that ring." When Solomon took the ring off to show Asmodeus he was still powerful without it, Asmodeus grabbed it, thus freeing himself and the other demons from bondage.

Another version has it the other way around. In this one, it was

Solomon who taunted Asmodeus, saying, "How can you demons say you are so powerful? Why just this little ring alone can hold you in bondage!" But Asmodeus cleverly replied, "If you take the ring off, sire, I'll show you that I'm still strong."

Either way, Asmodeus got the ring, and when he did he not only set himself and his friends free but he also ruled for several years in Solomon's place. In fact, some people say it was he and not Solomon who built the temple to Moloch. But eventually Solomon returned and got the magic ring back. When he did, he punished Asmodeus and the other demons by putting them in a black bottle, which he threw into a well. And there it remained till some Babylonians, looking for treasure, broke it and freed the demons, who returned to their old tricks.

Azazel is another infernal demon who goes back to the ancient Hebrews. He was probably a god at first; at least a goat was offered to him periodically to free people from their sins. Our word *scapegoat* comes from this practice: the high priest, his hands on the goat's head, confessed the sins of the people and then drove the goat into the wilderness to Azazel. The goat carried, the people believed, all their sins with it.

In the Book of Enoch, Azazel is said to have been one of the sons of God who, with the daughters of men, produced all demons. Some stories say he was their leader and was sent into the desert by God as punishment—as sin-laden scapegoats were later sent to him. As a demon, Azazel was responsible for teaching people the ways of war and of witchcraft, and he was at one time, with Samaël, an angel of death.

Obviously there are many more demons in hell than there is space to describe them here, but there's one more, Tutevillus, who deserves special mention. All demons had jobs, as you've seen by now; there were demons of gluttony, of murder, of jealousy, of the various sciences and arts, of vanity, of robbery, of philosophy, of hatred. Tutevillus was demon of gossiping in church!

Sunday after Sunday the faithful Tutevillus hied himself off to church with his trusty parchment to write down all the gossip that people whispered rudely during the sermon and the prayers. He didn't do this out of idle curiosity (though it must have been a fascinating job). According to the story, when the gossipers died and went to hell, as of course they must, the authorities looked up Tutevillus' notes and confronted the culprits with the very words they'd said in church.

Tutevillus' was a difficult job, apparently, for on one occasion, while he was perched on a ceiling beam listening to the whispers, he had so much to write down that he ran out of room on his parchment. He tried vigorously to stretch it but lost his balance and tumbled off the beam—much to the surprise, one imagines, of the people in the congregation, gossipers and nongossipers alike.

Like Satan, demons in general could shape-shift, and because of that it's often difficult to sort out their true shapes from their assumed ones. Some demonologists said demons had no basic shape at all but were airy spirits who had to "borrow" bodies if they wanted to be seen. Others were sure that demons manufactured the bodies they appeared in, using clouds and mist as raw materials and adding things like dirt, water, sulphur, wood, and, when needed, bones. Some demonologists said all demons were, like the Terrible Seven, neither male nor female—though most demons usually appeared as male.

Demons, like Satan, were often very cold to the touch. Many limped as Satan did, and had hooves and tails. Some smelled like goats—although not, of course, the fastidious Asmodeus. Many of hell's demons, like their Fertile Crescent ancestors, had basic shapes that were combinations of incompatible creatures: dogs, serpents, and birds; humans, fish, and frogs; and so forth. A demon needing to travel fast would sometimes change into a horse; if it was necessary to get into a locked room, a demon might change into air or an insect. Demons sometimes appeared riding on scary animals—a crocodile or a snake, for instance—and they frequently carried spears or birds of prey to make them look even more terrifying.

Sometimes, if it suited their purpose, demons chose to appear in normal human shape, as Satan usually did. Sometimes they even impersonated saints. Most of the time, though, demons appeared in the most horrible shape they could muster. Although St. Godric, a hermit in the twelfth century, occasionally saw a demon who looked like a real person, he was more frequently tormented by demons who looked like hideous animals or ugly dwarfs and who kept throwing him out of bed and beating him up.

One reason why demons usually looked horrible was, of course, because they liked scaring people. But a more important reason was self-protection. Demons were frequently bothered by sorcerers, the only mortals with power over them. Sorcerers made a habit of summoning demons—"calling them up" or "raising" them—and asking them, when they appeared, to do favors. Demons used horrible shapes and smells and sounds to discourage sorcerers from summoning them. Beelzebub, for example, used to take advantage of his Persian heritage and appear as a huge aggressive fly. Sometimes, however, demons went the other route and tried to look as harmless as possible, hoping to lull the sorcerer into a false sense of security so he could be easily tricked. Lucifer, for example, often appeared to sorcerers as an innocent boy.

When they were on earth, some demons—usually those descended from Semitic gods—liked to stay in dry desertlike places. Others, often those related to disease demons, preferred damp ones. All of them, however, were inclined to wander, endlessly seeking revenge for having been thrown out of heaven. Like Satan in *Paradise Lost*, most demons apparently felt the best way to get revenge was by harming human beings. One of their favorite techniques for doing this was possession (more about that later). Others, of course, were causing illness or insomnia, or stealing children, or making livestock stray, or even trying to keep treasure from falling into human hands. But even though Asmodeus once had a good laugh at a wizard who, for all his magic powers, was unaware he was sitting on a vast treasure trove, demons usually

didn't get much out of guarding treasure. One poor demon, asked to pay for a cask of wine he'd broken, complained that even if he knew where to find treasure he'd still have a hard time acquiring money to pay for what he'd done. Demons, he said, were only allowed to take what was lying around loose. Treasure, of course, was always locked up, so even its demon guards couldn't get at it.

When demons weren't causing mischief or disease or guarding treasure, if one believes the old tales, they were passing themselves off as great lovers, no doubt in order to recruit souls for hell. Women were visited at night by male demon lovers called incubi, and men were visited by succubi, Lilith's daughters. Incubi and succubi were especially common in medieval convents and monasteries. Some modern psychiatrists explain that by saying the lonely nuns and monks imagined them, out of a subconscious longing to be with the opposite sex.

Even if relationships between humans and incubi or succubi were imaginary, people believed that children were sometimes born of them. The magician Merlin, when he wasn't said to be Satan's son, was said to be the child of a lesser demon and a mortal. There were those who claimed that their personal and political enemies were the offspring of incubi or succubi. The Huns, for example, warlike nomads from Asia who terrorized Europe in the fourth and fifth centuries, were supposed to be the children of demons. Much later, Martin Luther's enemies said he was a demon child too. Some children born of demons, said demonologists, unlike Luther, the Huns, or Merlin, were in animal shape or even monster shape. Consequently, in the Middle Ages deformed babies and children who developed abnormally were sometimes thought to be the offspring of demons—as was a thirteenth-century boy who at the

Demons rounding up souls for hell. An illustration attributed to Albrecht Dürer.

*Hell's demons wearing some
of their weirder shapes.*

age of six months had all his teeth and was close to five feet tall!

Sometimes, in addition to producing children with mortals, demons were said to snatch babies from their mothers at birth and substitute their own babies—like the changelings fairies were supposed to leave in place of mortal children. In the early 1400s a group of demons supposedly manufactured devil babies out of stolen human infants. They formed lifeless bodies, it seems, out of a powder made from the dead infants and then crawled inside the bodies!

Obviously, since demons caused all these problems, the science of getting rid of them was very important. Sometimes demons could be lured into a trap with a saucer of milk, of all things, for bait. You could also sometimes get rid of a demon by paying tribute to it. Demons, believed some Celtic people in Britain, did not like to see plowed land, so farmers would leave sections of their property unplowed to please them. And because demons hated iron, some people hung a piece of an iron plow or a horseshoe over their front doors. Then, too, demons—despite their residence in hell—were afraid of fire. Farmers in the Scottish Hebrides paraded with lighted torches around their cattle to keep demons away. Various herbs were also good for scaring demons off: mugwort, garlic, rue, mullein, vervain, asafetida, St.-John's-wort. You could either wear these, scatter them on your floor, or tie them in bunches around your house.

There were even more familiar protective measures. Have you ever thrown salt over your left shoulder? If so, you were acting on two old folk beliefs: that demons hate salt (it is a preservative and demons like decay), and that demons stay on one's left side. Do you cover your mouth when you yawn? Sure, you're being polite—but a few centuries ago the reason why people did that was to keep demons from jumping in!

Sometimes people found they could scare a demon away with a face that was even more horrible than his or her own; sometimes they were even able to use the demon's own face, it was so ugly. Some demonologists said that was the true purpose of gargoyles, those grotesque carved creatures that decorated medieval churches. True, some folks claimed that gargoyles represented demons that had been driven out of the church building—but others said they were there to keep demons away by showing them their own ugliness. That was certainly the idea behind the use of mirrors as a form of demon prevention practiced, as you'll see in the next chapter, in non-European parts of the world.

6
Demons Far and Wide

WHEN HERNANDO CORTEZ, the Spanish explorer, conquered the Aztecs in the sixteenth century, he was horrified to see that the statues of their gods were bloodstained and that human hearts were lying near them. He expressed his shock to Montezuma, the conquered Aztec emperor, saying that he couldn't figure out how anyone as intelligent as Montezuma could think that such cruel creatures were gods. It was obvious, said Cortez, that they were actually demons, for they demanded human sacrifices; couldn't Montezuma see that?

Montezuma could not. His anger grew as he told Cortez that he was being disrespectful. Montezuma said that if he had thought Cortez would be so rude as to blaspheme, he would never have showed him his gods in the first place. It was the gods, Montezuma explained to Cortez, who gave the Aztecs all the good things of life; they deserved to have sacrifices made to them.

Though its details may not be 100 percent accurate, that story does illustrate the kind of misunderstanding that can occur when one culture meets another and is baffled by its customs and its values. The confusion about what was a god and what was a demon did not stop, as you can see, when the Fertile Crescent civilizations fell. It continued, in fact, right into modern times, when missionaries went into African and Asian countries and found gods who they felt were demonic.

The confusion is made even greater by the fact that there are two main kinds of demons in the world. First, there are those demons like Satan who are in some way connected with religion. Then there are what could be called "folklore demons," who have little to do with religion. Most of these are demons who cause a single kind of harm or discomfort: hunger demons, disease demons, demons of lonely places. The two kinds of demons often overlap—but if you think of, say, Asmodeus as a model for a "religious" demon, you'll probably begin to see the distinction. Asmodeus, after all, was too busy discharging his duties in hell, wearing fancy clothes, and chasing after women to bother about such petty activities as giving people tuberculosis!

Like Asmodeus, religious demons often had several jobs and many powers; folklore demons were more specialized. People in all parts of the world had hunger demons in their folklore—from the Scandinavians, who believed in a hunger demon they could get to eat their neighbors' livestock, to the Karens people of Africa, who believed in a hunger demon which was nothing more than a huge disembodied stomach. Vampires, those sophisticated undead creatures who have a tremendous appetite for blood, probably originated as hunger demons. So probably did ghouls—creatures who eat corpses.

There were also demons of fire, of storms, of dark places, of mountains and caves, of drought, and of cold. In China, a cold demon called the Ke-Mung, who had the shape of a man and the head of a dragon, was believed to cause rain. The Micmac Indians of Nova Scotia believed in cold demons called Chenoos who used dragons' horns for weapons and had ice for hearts. They could only be killed if their hearts were heated, but such a lot of water came from the melting ice that people who did a careless job of killing Chenoos could be drowned.

There have always been folklore demons of treacherous mountain passes, of bottomless lakes, of terrifying whirlpools, of dangerous marshes. In France there was a mountain lake which Gervase of

Tilbury, a medieval chronicler, said had a demon palace in its depths. Anyone who disturbed the water by throwing a rock into the lake apparently disturbed the occupant of the palace too—at least a huge storm raged the moment the water rippled.

Almost all folklore demons could cause storms, of course—like one of St. Godric's tormentors who spewed out black clouds from his mouth and raised a fearful flood. Demon-caused storms were so common in England in the fifteenth and sixteenth centuries that clergymen rang their church bells whenever a bad storm struck, just in case there were demons around to be driven away.

In both European and Arabian countries, folklore demons who didn't inhabit dangerous places sometimes lived in a plant called a mandrake, which for centuries was an important ingredient in spells. The mandrake probably got its supernatural reputation from its root, which looks oddly like a human being. Because of that, people used to think a demon lived in each mandrake and that the plant, or its demon, shrieked when it was uprooted. Anyone hearing a mandrake shriek, it was widely believed, would go mad or die or be attacked by the demon.

Most demons, folklore and otherwise, preferred the north to the south, as did Satan, which is why the northern part of some graveyards is left unblessed and suicides are buried there. Some old churches were built with their doors facing south to make it as hard as possible for demons to enter.

One of the most common of folklore demons was the nightmare —the demon who caused bad dreams. We know today that dreams are normal and even necessary to psychological health—but think how terrifying they must have been to people who didn't realize they were "all in one's mind." Have you ever woken up from a dream and for a minute been confused, not quite sure where your dream stopped and reality began? Suppose you didn't know that dreams are little more than mental movies, vivid but not real. You might very well think, as people did long ago, that they were actual supernatural adventures, caused by an evil spirit—Mahr (or Mara), the dread nightmare demon.

"Mahr rode me all night long," was the way restless sleepers often told their families they'd been dreaming. "And when I woke up my room was full of mist. I dreamed I clutched the spirit, but it changed to straw. Look, when I woke up, I had this same piece of straw in my hand!"

Usually the Mahr appeared as a beautiful but treacherous woman, but sometimes she appeared as a man, an ugly animal, or a dwarf; it depended, of course, on what the dream was about. The Mahr was treacherous because she sometimes killed sleepers. People who died in their sleep, especially young ones, were said to have been murdered by the nightmare demon. People who felt a sense of suffocation while they slept or when they woke in the middle of the night would say that Mahr was sitting on them.

You could capture a Mahr by putting something in the keyhole of your room so she couldn't get out in the morning. You could also get rid of her by crossing yourself, or by asking her who she really was. That, apparently, frightened her, for if a person questioned her she usually disappeared—till the next time the person had a bad dream.

Unlike the Mahr, who usually operated alone, the major religious demons of many different cultures were locked in endless battle with the forces of good, like Ahriman and Ormazd, Satan and God. One of the most vivid of these good-evil battles comes from the Hindu tradition of India.

Long, long ago, according to one version of the ancient Indian myth, the gods, or Devas, lost their supply of their favorite drink, amrita. Not only was amrita truly wonderful to taste, but it also was the source of the Devas' immortality; without it, they would have to die like anyone else.

The Devas, along with the Asuras (serpents), sought high and low for the missing amrita. At length they decided to seek it in the ocean. To make a "hole" in the water, they realized, they would have to stir the ocean, thus creating a whirlpool. A mountain, they decided, would make a good "spoon," so they toppled one into the sea. One of the Asuras, a great serpent named Vásuki, twirled the mountain by coiling and uncoiling his body around it. Soon, to everyone's relief, the amrita appeared.

Everything had gone smoothly so far, but now the Asuras, no doubt because the amrita would not have been found without their help, claimed the drink for themselves. An argument followed; the Devas refused to give the amrita up and there seems to have been no question of sharing. Quickly, one of the Devas changed himself into a beautiful woman and distracted the Asuras just long enough to allow the Devas to drink the amrita. He distracted all the Asuras but one, that is: Ráhu, who was too smart to be tricked. Ráhu realized what was happening and filled his mouth with the immortalizing liquid. The moon and sun saw what he was doing, however, and cried out a warning; one of the Devas reacted quickly enough to slice off Ráhu's head. But there was just enough amrita in Ráhu's mouth to make his head immortal. Angry at being betrayed, Ráhu's immortal head went up to the sky, bent on revenge against the moon and sun. Every time there is an eclipse, it is Ráhu swallowing one of those who betrayed him. Since he has no body, though, the swallowed moon or sun soon reappears, and the cycle starts all over again.

Ever since this incident, the Devas and the Asuras have been locked in war, still over the amrita. Over and over again the Devas have won, but the Asuras, who have become more demonic with each round of the battle, never stop trying to outsmart them and get the precious drink for themselves.

More horrible than Ráhu, but probably related to the Asuras, were the Indian demons called the Rāksasas. Eating the sun and moon is one thing, but the Rāksasas were cannibals, redheaded demons with huge mouths and pointed ears. Anyone who met a Rāksasa at midnight, when they were strongest, was doomed to be devoured. They weren't always easy to recognize, for despite their distinctive basic appearance, they could shape-shift. They frequently changed into dogs or apes but they especially liked to appear as beautiful men or women so they could easily lure people into their clutches. When they were more interested in frightening people than enticing them, however, they appeared as humans with three heads, five feet, and hands with horns on them. One of their nastiest habits was that of snatching people up when they were praying. Another was attacking pregnant women. Some Rāksasas specialized in attacking people of certain ages. One kind, for example, liked children and teenagers; another liked adults. One of their favorite tricks was to hide on a forkful of food. Anyone who ate a Rāksasa hidden in this way could become possessed or sometimes even crazy.

The greatest Rāksasa of all time was Ravana, their (in some pictures) ten-headed leader, who lived with his demons on what is today the island of Sri Lanka. Ravana had a long-standing feud with the gods and once forced them all to work as his slaves. Though the gods eventually escaped, they could do nothing to punish Ravana, because earlier the god Brahma, in return for Ravana's worship, had made it impossible for the gods to harm him.

The gods' revenge came much later, but it came. In order to create someone who could conquer Ravana, the god Vishnu cut himself into quarters. From one of those quarters came the great hero Rama, who, with an army of monkeys, fought long and hard against Ravana. During the course of the war, Ravana captured Sita, Rama's wife, and tried to force her to marry him. She refused, even though the cruel Rāksasa said he would eat her if she didn't become his wife. Sita's bravery was rewarded, though, for Rama and Hanuman, the monkey general, finally saved her. There followed many more battles, but at last Rama shot Ravana with an arrow given him by Brahma, and the cruel demon leader breathed his last.

Ravana approaching Sita

A prisoner of the ten-headed Ravana, Sita is guarded by the Rāksasas.

After that, the remaining Rāksasas became weaker, even a little timid. They spent most of their time living in trees and, although they were still strongest at midnight, about the worst they could do was cause stomach trouble or prey on corpses. When they appeared it was most often as feeble old women—not as the terrifying demons of earlier days.

Of all the individual demonic beings in India, perhaps the most famous is Mara (not to be confused with the nightmare demon). Mara is famous because he tried to tempt the great Prince Siddhartha, who founded Buddhism, a major Oriental religion.

The night that Prince Siddhartha (later called the Buddha, or Enlightened One), left his palace to seek truth as a humble monk, he was approached by King Mara, god of death and of love. Mara felt threatened by the prince's plan, for he knew that if Siddhartha was successful in his quest, Mara would no longer have power over him or over his followers. He must have guessed that these followers would one day be numerous, for he offered Siddhartha the whole world if he would only give up his search. But Siddhartha refused, explaining that searching for religious truth was better than gaining riches.

The search, however, was long and wearisome. As part of it, Siddhartha fasted, and when he had become pale and thin from self-denial, Mara approached him again. This time he pretended to sympathize with the prince. "You are so thin, Siddhartha," he said, "so pale and so weak. You will die soon if you do not eat. Think, oh, just think of the great feasts you could have if you returned to the world! Would they not sit better in your stomach than the pain of emptiness?"

But Siddhartha, despite his hunger, was stronger than Mara thought he was. Once again he refused, calling Mara wicked for tempting him.

Mara left, defeated for the moment, but he returned a third time. Before he himself arrived, he sent his three daughters to Siddhartha while he sat under the famous bo, or fig, tree where he eventually achieved his goal of enlightenment. Mara's daughters, Love, Anger, and Desire (or Pleasure, Passion, and Desire, as they are sometimes called), went up to the prince in their fanciest clothes and danced to tempt him, but Siddhartha chased them away.

Mara then assembled his army, who assumed the most fearful

shapes imaginable. He himself increased his size, becoming an enormous monster, and, mounted on an elephant that was a thousand miles tall, he led his demons to the bo tree. They and the floods and earthquakes they released managed to scare away the gods who were guarding the prince, but even so, they could not get close to Siddhartha. No matter how hard they pressed their attack, they found themselves powerless. Even the burning ashes they hurled at the prince turned to flowers. At last Mara unleashed a weapon strong enough to break mountains—but flowers, deceptively fragile, sprang up and protected him. Then a brave and lovely spirit came to the prince's aid and released a flood which swept Mara and his demon army away.

Mara, unlike most evil gods and demons, admitted his defeat. More than that, he acknowledged the Buddha's goodness and predicted that he would become the teacher of all creatures, even demons.

In China there were so many demons that people believed, as Paracelsus had, that they were constantly surrounded by them. There were even demons hiding in furniture, they thought. The shapes of Chinese demons varied as much as those of demons in any other land. Some were almost human, and at least one group of them, those who served the kings of hell, had hornlike bumps on their heads.

Chinese demons caused all manner of evil and sorrowful events. They brought fire, disease, crop failures, and storms. They caused convulsions, stole souls, and killed people, often by drowning. If a child had a convulsion and its mother feared a demon had taken its soul, she would hold up one of the child's garments and try to call the stolen soul back into it. Some parents, fearing that demons might attack their babies, fastened mirrors to infants' heads. This was also done in Guinea, Africa, and for the same reason: the demons were so ugly, people thought, that they would run away as soon as they saw themselves in the mirrors.

One could sometimes frighten Chinese demons away with fire-crackers or with magic charms placed in strategic locations. One could also protect oneself if one burned an antidemon charm, made tea from the ashes, and drank the tea. Intelligent and honest folk, some people believed, had an easier time defeating demons than others. Two brothers called the "peach men" who lived in ancient times must have been both brilliant and scrupulously honest, for they could catch demons by the simple method of hanging a charm in a peach tree. Whenever they caught a demon, they fed it to a tiger. But most people were reluctant to kill demons, for some of them, as soon as they were dead, simply transformed themselves into demons of another breed—usually worse than the kind they'd been originally.

China was one of the places where nineteenth-century missionaries labeled a good many ancient gods and ancestor spirits as demons. Nonetheless some of the spirits that missionaries called demons were worshiped by the people as gods and used by them for predicting the future. It is true that Christian Chinese also tended to call them demons, at least when they were talking with missionaries, but chances are that to non-Christians many of these creatures were more divine than demonic and only did evil deeds when they were displeased.

In both China and Japan people believed in fox-demons or fox-witches—evil, usually female spirits who were shaped like foxes but who upon occasion turned themselves into beautiful women. The usual purpose of this was so they could marry mortal men. Surprisingly enough, fox-demons often lived with their husbands happily for years before their true shapes were discovered.

Fox-demons, though, were very specialized. A more conventional demon in Japanese folklore was the Oni. Actually, there were several kinds of Oni. Some were vampires or cannibals; others were giants or goblins. Their usual jobs were to cause storms and to punish evildoers. When a wicked person died, it was believed that an Oni would appear in a flaming cart to take his or her soul to hell.

Oni were of various shapes and sizes, although many had flat faces, wiry hair, and odd-looking three-toed feet with pointed nails. Some had three eyes. The kind of Oni who punished evildoers could often be recognized by its horns and by its skin color, which was apt to be blue or pink. An Oni's skin was readily visible, for most of them wore only a tigerskin loincloth. Oni were considered very dangerous, but if you found one with a magic mallet, you might be able, like the princess in this story, to get any wish you asked for:

It seems that a middle-aged man and his wife had long prayed for a child and finally were so desperate they said to the gods, "Please send us a son, even if he is only an inch tall." The gods honored that wish, and soon little Issun-bōshi was born.

Despite the boy's tininess—a normal person could hold him in the

A *Japanese demon*

palm of one hand—he was brave and intelligent and his parents had few qualms when he grew up and went off to the capital to seek his fortune. Soon he was employed as a servant in a great house, where he became the close friend of the young princess who lived there.

One day, when Issun-bōshi and the princess were on their way home after visiting a temple, an Oni sprang up at them out of nowhere. He looked greedily at the princess. "Aha! What a tasty morsel," he said. (He was clearly a cannibal-type Oni.) "Prepare to be eaten."

Issun-bōshi, who was many times braver than his size would suggest, gathered his little body for a spring. With all his strength he leaped into the great gaping mouth of the Oni. Issun-bōshi's sword was only a pin, but he laid about with it as if it were the stoutest blade in all Japan and he the bravest samurai warrior, delivering pinpricks as fast as he could to the Oni's mouth and nose.

"Begone, fly!" muttered the Oni, swatting at Issun-bōshi, who hid behind a tooth and thrust again. Faster and faster he attacked, till the Oni could stand it no longer and fled with a great roar, forgetting the princess who had seemed such a tasty morsel only a few minutes earlier. Before he left, however, the demon sneezed such a sneeze that Issun-bōshi was blown out of his mouth and onto the ground. Luckily, he landed unharmed.

"Oh, thank you," cried the princess, picking Issun-bōshi up and gently brushing him off. "You have saved my life!" she sighed. "Issun-bōshi, how I wish that I could repay you."

It was then that she spotted the Oni's mallet, which he'd left behind in his haste to escape the pain of Issun-bōshi's attack. With a cry of joy, the princess— who knew that Onis' mallets were magic —picked the instrument up and swung it high over her head. "Magic mallet, magic mallet," she said, "make my friend Issun-bōshi grow till he reaches normal size."

Immediately the tiny creature grew. In a matter of minutes, he was able to look down on the princess and smile. Then he took her gently in his arms to thank her properly. And, as you've probably guessed, it was not long before these two good friends were married, ready to live a long and happy life free from Oni and all other evil beings.

It's a long journey from Japan to the Arab countries, but it would not be long either in distance or time for those most durable of all demons, the mighty djinn. You may already know the *Arabian Nights* story of Aladdin, who had a magic lamp with which he could call a djinni, or genie, as this creature is sometimes called. However, if most of what you know of djinn (that's the plural) is what you've seen on the TV situation comedy "I Dream of Jeannie," you may need a little more information. Here's another *Arabian Nights* story to fill in some of the gaps:

Once upon a time there was an old fisherman who was very poor. Besides himself, he had a wife and three children to support. Sometimes his net brought up enough fish to feed his family and sometimes it brought up more than enough, so he could sell the excess for cooking pots and clothes and other necessities. But sometimes the fisherman's net brought up nothing useful at all, and then he and his family had to go hungry.

For three days now, that had been the case, and the poor fisherman was close to despair. On the first day, all he'd caught was the corpse of a donkey, which tore his net in many places. The next day, after he'd mended his net, he caught nothing but a basket of gravel. And on the third day, all he got was mud and shells.

On the fourth day, when he tugged at his net, it was heavier than ever. Still, the fisherman told himself he must not hope for fish. The donkey had been heavy and so had the gravel and the mud and shells, so there was no reason to believe that this catch would be any better. Indeed, as he tugged and heaved and tugged, he found himself wishing for a less heavy load, not only because it would be easier to pull in but also because a lighter load might mean fish at last.

But as the fisherman had feared, this was another useless catch— just a large copper jar sealed with lead. When he picked the jar up, though, the fisherman found it was heavy—so heavy he realized there must be something in it, maybe even something he could sell. He lifted the jar to his ear and shook it, but heard no sound. Then he pried its cover off with his knife and looked inside. Nothing. The jar was dark and seemed empty; in fact, when he turned it upside down, nothing fell out. Disappointed, the fisherman turned the jar upright again and prepared to pack up his net and leave. Suddenly he saw a wisp of smoke, and then more, and then a cloud, pouring from the open jar—so much smoke that he had to leap back to get out of its way.

Faster and faster came the smoke till it filled the sky, while the poor fisherman trembled with fright. Imagine how he felt when the smoke grew denser, pulling in on itself as if trying to form into a shape—which indeed is exactly what it did. In less time than it takes to tell, the smoke had molded itself into an enormous djinni.

The fisherman was so terrified at first that he couldn't move. But when the djinni spoke, his words were so ridiculous that the fisherman took courage. "Master," said the djinni, "great King Solomon, master, pardon me! Oh, pardon me, I will not defy you anymore!"

"What is this?" said the fisherman, now feeling quite brave. "King Solomon has been dead for eighteen hundred years! How can it be that you call on him? Who are you anyway and how came you inside that jar?"

"And who are you?" demanded the djinni, his formerly whining voice now fierce. "Who are you who speaks to me so rudely? Speak with respect or I shall kill you!"

The fisherman began to feel frightened again, but he answered the djinni bravely. "Kill me!" he exclaimed. "Didn't I just release you from that jar? Do I not deserve thanks instead of killing?"

"Well, perhaps," admitted the djinni begrudgingly, "but unhappily for you that doesn't mean I shall spare you. However," he added grandly, "you may have one favor of me—one only."

"What kind of favor?" asked the fisherman, hoping the djinni could free him and his family from poverty.

But no such luck. "You may," said the djinni in his booming voice, "decide in what way you would like to die."

"I wouldn't like to die at all," sputtered the fisherman, now more frightened than ever. "Besides, why should I? I have done nothing wrong!"

"I cannot help that," replied the djinni. "There is nothing I can do about it. Long ago I joined with the spirits who went against heaven's will. And I was one of two who defied the great Solomon. Even when I was brought before Solomon I would not accept his power, so he put me in that copper jar. He sealed the top with lead as you have seen and had the jar thrown into the sea. At first I thought if anyone let me out I would make that person comfortably rich. After a hundred years I decided I would give whoever freed me many tons of gold and silver and other great minerals. In the next hundred years I decided I would make my liberator a great king and give him three wishes every day. But after three hundred years when no one came to free me from that stuffy jar I could no longer think of rewards. I became so angry I vowed to kill whoever freed me. I decided I would grant that person one favor only: his choice of how he wanted to die. I cannot help it, my friend, that it was you who were the instrument of my liberation. It is only fate that it is upon you that my wrath must fall."

"But that isn't fair!" shouted the fisherman. "Why me? It is an unjust plan. I cannot tell you how unjust it is. Think of my wife and children if not of me or of justice. They will starve without me. Please grant me my life, O djinni," the fisherman begged. "In return, I am sure heaven will reward you."

But the djinni still refused, and nothing the fisherman could say made him change his mind.

"Very well," said the fisherman, realizing he would have to outsmart the djinni. "Perhaps it is the will of Allah that I die. But since these are my last moments on earth, surely you will answer one question for me truthfully so I may go to my death knowing more than I do now."

"Well," asked the djinni impatiently, "what is the question?"

"You must answer it truthfully," said the fisherman.

"Yes, yes," said the djinni. "Just ask it. What is it?"

"Were you truly in this little jar?" asked the fisherman. "Truly? Do you swear by Allah that you were?"

"Certainly," said the djinni without hesitation. "I swear it. Now, about your death . . ."

The fisherman shook his head. "I would like to believe you," he said slowly, "but I find I cannot. You see, you are so large and the jar is so small in comparison! How is it possible for someone of your great and noble size to fit into so small a space?"

"I assure you it is possible," said the djinni. "How can you doubt me when I have sworn upon Allah?"

"Ah," said the fisherman, "that is true. Let us say that I know not how I can doubt you but nonetheless it seems that I do. Perhaps you are only a dream. Perhaps you only *appeared* to come out of the jar. There are many possibilities." He shook his head again. "No, djinni," he said, "I do not see how I can ever believe you—unless, of course, I were to see you in the jar again. Perhaps if you showed me how you fit into the jar . . . Yes, I feel sure of it! If I actually saw you in the jar, I would certainly have to believe you."

Immediately the djinni turned to smoke which, as before, first filled the sky and then gathered in on itself and poured back into the jar. When there was no more smoke in the sky, a voice from inside the jar said, "Well, fisherman, do you believe me now?"

And at that moment the fisherman, who had made himself ready, clapped the cover on the jar and cried triumphantly, "Now I have you, djinni! Now perhaps you would like to tell *me* how *you* would like to die!"

The djinni fought and struggled and thrashed around inside the jar for such a long time that the fisherman said, as if to himself, "I guess it would be better for me to return this old jar to the sea."

When he heard that, the djinni shouted, "No! No, master! Listen, I was only joking before about killing you."

"Joking indeed," said the fisherman severely. "I begged you to save me and you refused. I will not spare you now. Into the sea with you."

Then the djinni, thinking to influence the fisherman, told a long story about a great and noble king who spared the life of someone under similar circumstances. After that they argued awhile longer, but finally the fisherman agreed to let the djinni out of the jar when the djinni promised to free him from poverty.

The fisherman took the lid off the jar, and smoke poured out until once again the djinni stood before him. As soon as he became solid again, the djinni kicked the jar into the sea and laughed so boisterously that the fisherman feared he had made a terrible mistake.

"Do not be afraid, fisherman," said the djinni. "I will keep my word. I just wanted to make sure that cursed jar was well out of the way first. Now, pick up your net and come with me."

The djinni led the fisherman far away to a mountain, and then from the mountain to a plain, and then across the plain to a lake the fisherman had never seen before. "Cast your net here," he told the fisherman, "and you will be rewarded." With some doubt, the fisherman did as he was told. Soon he caught four beautiful fish, one red, one white, one yellow, and one blue. "Take these fish to the sultan," said the djinni, "and he will pay you well for them—so well you will be able to buy enough for your family to eat and fine clothes to wear besides. You may return here every day, but once a day only, to catch four such fish for the sultan. And by and by you will see what you will see." With those mysterious words the djinni stamped his foot, and the ground, as if obeying a command, opened up and took him inside.

The fisherman, though he was puzzled, did everything the djinni had said. The sultan did indeed pay vast sums for the fish that first day. But alas, when the sultan's cook tried to prepare the fish for eating, spirits appeared and threw them on the floor, charred and unfit to eat. Day after day, however, the fisherman was able to sell his strange catch to the sultan, and day after day the fish were charred and destroyed. At last the sultan decided to go to the lake to see where the strange fish came from; perhaps then he could find out why he was never allowed to eat them.

The sultan, after careful investigation, learned that the fish were really the enchanted inhabitants of an old city, long ago destroyed by a wicked queen. He was able to lift the spell and set the city and its grateful inhabitants to rights again. Then he awarded the fisherman a huge fortune, making good the djinni's promise—for if it had not been for the fisherman, the lost city would never have been found.

Djinn are mentioned in the Koran, the sacred book of the religion Islam. As you can see from the fisherman's story, they weren't by any means completely bad. In fact, there were good djinn as well as evil djinn, and also more or less neutral ones like the one the fisherman found. Djinn in general were considered halfway between humans and angels—not as good as angels, but better than most humans. Like Iblis, who was usually considered their leader— yes, the same Iblis you read about earlier in this book—they were created by Allah out of fire before human beings; originally it was they who ruled the world. One story says that after a couple of thousand years of ruling they became corrupt and rebelled against Allah, so Allah sent Iblis to drive them into exile. The more common story, however, is that it was Iblis himself, angry about the creation of Adam, who led the rebellion, and that it was the angels who drove both him and the djinn into exile.

Djinn had marvelous magic powers and were especially good at building. It was even said that they built the pyramids of Egypt— and, as you may already have guessed from the fisherman's story, in the Koran it was djinn, not Asmodeus and his crew, who helped Solomon build his Temple at Jerusalem.

Djinn weren't restricted to human shape or smoke shape; they could turn into anything they liked. Good djinn especially liked the shapes of snakes or toads and for that reason some people were careful not to harm snakes or toads that lived near their homes. Some djinn were rather shy and preferred to stay invisible, but if a cock crowed suddenly for no reason, people knew there was a djinni someplace nearby. No one has made an entirely accurate djinn census, but some estimates of their number run as high as 24 million —a number made more formidable by the idea that djinn some- times married and had children. Many djinn children, people be- lieved, were invisible, but even when they were not they usually had magic powers of some kind.

Djinn were usually very large, like the gigantic one in the fisherman's story, and the evil ones were truly terrifying. One of the most widely known evil djinn, probably because it haunted Europe and England as well as the Arabian countries, was the ghul, or ghoul, who fed on corpses. The Arabian ghoul has been pictured as a sort of birdlike being with a body that looks rather like a nut, and legs a little like cucumbers—but like other djinn, ghouls could shape-shift, so you could never be sure if you were faced with one or not. That wouldn't matter much if they only ate corpses, but ghouls also drove people senseless and then tore them apart to eat their flesh. They often lived in cemeteries, as might be expected, but when they were hungry for fresher meat they haunted other lonely places.

Another scary evil djinni—and the most intelligent—was the

afrit. The really terrifying thing about this demon was that you could never be sure what it was going to do next. One minute an afrit would look and act like a harmless human being—and the next minute it would turn into a roaring lion and devour whomever it had been talking to. Afrits also had a reputation for being the most cruel djinn—although another group of Arabian demons, the shei-tans, were sometimes given that distinction instead. Sheitans (or seitanes) specialized in stealing children and in making people go insane.

In the Moslem Segeju tribe on the coast of what is now Tanzania, East Africa, the people believed in demons very like the djinn, no doubt because their culture mingled both Moslem and African beliefs. To the Segeju, however, djinn were sea demons who controlled fish and the motion of the waves. Segeju fishermen made offerings to djinn in order to make sure they had a good catch. The Segeju also believed in demons called shetani. (*Shetani* is a Swahili word related, of course, to the Arabian word *sheitan*. Both probably come from the same Semitic word *Satan* comes from.) Although the shetani caused illness and accidents, they were not terribly evil. They did, however, fall from heaven with the Segejus' chief devil—Iblisi!

The forerunners of these djinnlike creatures, some demonologists think, were the zimwi, who were probably the original African demons and who, under the influence of foreigners, eventually came to be called djinn, shetani, and finally devils or demons. People in various parts of Africa believed in zimwi and creatures with similar names. In Sierra Leone, for example, many stories were told about the tricks the zimwi played when they changed their shapes. In one, a zimwi became, of all things, a stone with a beard growing on it. Whenever anyone commented on this phenomenon out loud, the zimwi struck the person unconscious.

The cannibalistic izumu of the Bantu-speaking peoples in south-ern Africa was probably of the same general class of demons, as was the ilimu of the Kikuyu tribe in Kenya. The ilimu, another people-eater, was usually an animal who took on the shape of a person. Some ilimu had only one foot in the right place; the other was at the back of its neck. Another man-beast-demon was the irimu of the East African Chaga people. The irimu usually had a leopard's shape —but once a very wicked man turned into one, and when he did, bushes sprouted all over his body! He made himself valuable to his friends by eating their enemies, and as a reward someone freed him by burning the bushes off him. Another weird and monstrous demon in Africa was the aigamuchat, believed in by the Hottentots of the Kalahari Desert. This creature wore its eyes on its feet. The only way it could keep track of where it was going was by crawling with one foot up in the air!

Tired of reading about all these outlandish monsters? If not, here are a few more for you, in a very brief, very incomplete

DICTIONARY OF DEMONS

• *Als*—Armenian childbirth demon, probably related to the Alu of the Fertile Crescent. This demon, half human and half beast, was as horrible as Lilith at her most terrifying. It had shaggy hair and fiery eyes, could be either male or female, and lived in damp places or in the corners of houses. The Als, who usually carried scissors as weapons, attacked and strangled women in childbirth, along with their babies. They also stole babies two months before they were due to be born and gave them as special presents to their king. If a baby was born blind or deformed it was thought that an Als was probably responsible. If a woman fainted when she had given birth, people sometimes suspected an Als was near. Once in a while they would try to save the mother by exposing her baby to the elements as an offering to the Als. An easier protective measure was to surround the mother with iron objects.

• *Ankou*—Breton death demon: a skeleton. She called out to

those who lay dying at night, telling them to drive away with her in her cart—a bit the way the allegorical figure of Death took people away in medieval plays.

• *Bihlweisen*—German demons who dried up cows' milk and made them slowly sicken. Farmers washed their cows with wild cabbage boiled in wine to prevent this.

• *Cootchie*—a disease demon of Central Australia. He could be chased away by whacking the earth with a kangaroo tail. Another Australian disease demon, Biami, who caused smallpox, also taught people songs.

• *Didis*—demons, part monkey and part man, who haunted the mountains of Guiana, South America. They lay in wait, with fierce jaguars, for people who dared climb Mount Roraima. Also on Mount Roraima was a camoodi, a demon who enveloped and destroyed anyone who dared to climb to the top.

• *Hiisi*—Finnish wind demon. A bit like Pazuzu, this demon rode his horse through the sky with his dogs, cats, and monsters following close behind. His purpose: to bring death and disease.

• *Maya Danawa*—a Balinese demon who long ago was wounded by the gods near the Petanu River. Superstition had it that if the river's water was used for watering rice, the rice would spew forth her blood.

• *Miru*—a South Seas hunger demon. She grabbed souls before their bodies were dead, and killed, cooked, and ate them.

• *Mother Khön-ma*—a Tibetan goddess, the supervisor of demons. To keep her demons away, people would put out a display of jewels, precious metals, food, a ram's skull, and pictures of a couple and a house. Then, if a priest offered her the food and begged that she keep her demons to herself, her demons might be fooled into thinking the pictures were real and would bother them instead of people.

• *Nains*—Breton treasure demons. They were dark with red eyes and the legs of goats. Anyone who could figure out their alphabet was given the power of finding any treasure no matter where it was hidden.

• *Painters*—devil-panthers who lurked near the Mississippi River. They ate people and then afterward forced their spirits to obey them. Among their neighbors were invisible demons who rode on the shoulders of people who had made pacts with the Devil.

• *Penanggalan*—Malayan female vampire-demon, consisting of only a head and a stomach. This demon's bloody diet was limited to babies, children, and women in childbirth.

• *Pretas*—Siamese hunger demons. They were twelve miles tall but invisible because they were so thin.

• *Ran*—a Scandinavian sea goddess. She pulled ships to their destruction and caught drowned sailors in nets, which is why she was sometimes considered demonic. But when she carried the sailors off to her underwater palace she fed them on lobster and other deep-sea delicacies!

• *Sedna*—Eskimo underworld goddess. Sedna, with a crew of disease demons, came into the upper world whenever the ice melted and started to break up. She was the hardest demon to drive away and would not go back to the underworld unless she was harpooned.

• *Tsar Morskoi*—a Russian water demon. His swan-shaped daughters controlled the tides, and his water sprites drowned people who swam without wearing a cross. They also stole the catch of any fisherman who saved a person trying to commit suicide by drowning. Why? Because the souls of such people became water sprites themselves.

• *Uehuella-chagui* (Lame Foot)—a South African Indian demon. This demon could be recognized by its footprints. It was a good idea to watch out for it, because if you didn't recognize its prints, there was no way you'd know it was there; Lame Foot was a creature of many harmless-looking disguises. It killed anyone it could catch.

• *Will-o'-the-Wisp*—folklore name for the phosphorescence that sometimes shows over swamps. Will was believed to be a demonic being who led people astray with his light until they were sucked into the boggy mud and drowned.

But stop! The demons are crowding in again, trying to make the dictionary longer, demanding space between the entries, clamoring, as usual, to be heard. Even some of hell's demons are here, shouting and gesturing. There is Amaymon, King of the East, and Marbas, a lion-shaped president in hell, and Bclcthon, his horse, all demanding equal time and complaining that they have not yet been mentioned . . .

It is time to call the sorcerers in to control them!

7

Goetry:
Calling, Commanding,
Controlling Demons

ARE YOU PURE IN HEART and is your conscience clear? Is your courage unshakable? Can you withstand horror, temptation, ugliness, foul smells, attacks by monstrous beasts, tricks, and lies? If so, you have some of the basic requirements for practicing goetic, or "black," magic—the kind of magic that uses demons, summoned up from hell, to work its spells.°

Does that seem odd? Why should you have to be pure if your purpose is to give orders to the impure? As Eliphas Lévi, a nineteenth-century occultist, said, "We must overcome them [demons] in their strength without ever being overcome by their weakness." Any sorcerer who hoped to control demons had to be better than they were. In fact, he (women were apparently not allowed to perform the elaborate rituals necessary for summoning demons) had to be well-nigh perfect—even religious. Again, that may seem odd, since both religious and civil authorities in Judeo-Christian countries outlawed this kind of magic, but most sorcerers said they were not doing anything wrong. They felt they could ask God's help in raising demons because they rarely asked the demons to do anything they considered evil—in fact, most sorcerers claimed their

° Or which uses dead people. Necromancy, in which a sorcerer raises a dead person to make him or her prophesy, is usually included in goetic magic also.

purpose was to control them and force them to perform various relatively harmless tasks. In fact, one of the reasons sorcerers gave for keeping their rituals carefully guarded was to keep them from falling into the hands of truly evil people who, by abusing goetic secrets, might unleash the dread power of hell's demons upon the unsuspecting world.

The most usual purpose of summoning demons was to force them to tell where treasure was hidden—or sometimes where stolen goods had been stashed away. Occasionally a sorcerer called on a demon to assist him or a client in a love affair, to punish an enemy, or to get political power or a good job. Sometimes demons were asked to assist in noble public works—like those bridges Satan helped build. Only very rarely—at least according to the sorcerers —were demons asked to assist at real crimes, like murder.

In order to summon demons, a sorcerer had to follow the directions given in a grimoire—a book describing the rituals of goetic magic. You might expect most grimoires to be very old but, although a few really are and others claim to be, most of them date only from the sixteenth or seventeenth century, a time when, because of the Inquisition, Church authorities were very anxious to find people who were practicing evil magic.

One grimoire, called *The Red Book of Magic*, was supposed to have belonged to the Devil himself. It was said to be so powerful that anyone who read it had to wear an iron headband for protection! King Solomon himself was credited with having written one of the most famous grimoires, *The Key of Solomon*, and he supposedly contributed to many others. Demonologists, however, think it very unlikely that he did. One reason people thought he had was, of course, Solomon's reputation for being able to handle demons. Another reason was probably the association of Solomon with the Cabala, an old Hebrew work, based somewhat on Scriptures, of occult mystical religious philosophy. Solomon lived and died long before its time, but since the Cabala was mysterious to all except the few scholars who understood it, and since it described demons and gave apparently magical meanings to numbers, letters, and names, it seemed logical to outsiders to connect it with Solomon and both with goetic magic. In truth, however, it is unlikely that either Solomon or the Cabala had much to do with goetry; the Cabala, in fact, forbade it.

The rituals and the preparations for the rituals varied tremendously from grimoire to grimoire, but one thing most of them stressed, as did the Cabala, was the importance of names, in accordance with the ancient belief that to know a creature's name was to be able to control the creature. It was vital for this reason to know all the names and nicknames of the demons one dealt with. In order to control demons it was also vital to know all the names used for God. True, both the Cabala and the Church forbade the use of God's names in goetry—but, said the sorcerers, demons were subject to God's power, and one couldn't control them unless one could use God's names in goetic ritual. Even the demons had to use God's name—as in the following oath from a medieval grimoire, to be taken by the demon Lucifer:

> We Lucifer, and all beforementioned and following spirits, swear to you, to almighty God through Jesus Christ of Nazarus, the crucified one, our conqueror, that we will faithfully perform everything written in this book: also never to do you any harm, either to your body or your soul, and to execute everything immediately and without refusing.

Even though summoned demons swore such oaths, and sorcerers took many precautions to keep themselves from being harmed, sorcerers still had to be extraordinarily brave in order to face demons in all the horrible shapes they assumed when they appeared. There was no place for timidity in goetic magic, for demons would try every trick they knew to avoid serving sorcerers and would do their best to hurt anyone who summoned them. Before starting any ritual, a goetic sorcerer always drew a circle around himself, and as long as he stayed inside it and the demons stayed outside, he was safe. But the demons would still try everything in their power to lure the sorcerer out of the circle or to get into it themselves; they would cause terrifying storms and would exhibit their most hideous shapes, smells, and noises—or their most beautiful. One slip, one false move or word on the sorcerer's part and any demon would instantly be able to unleash all his or her infernal power against the sorcerer and destroy him. Because of this, sorcerers had to prepare carefully for every ceremony they performed.

According to many grimoires, the sorcerer planning to call up a demon must stay away from women for a certain period of time before the ceremony. He must eat sparingly beforehand and only at certain times of day; he should recite a formula, like a grace, before eating. Some grimoires also required that the sorcerer sleep as little as possible before a goetic ceremony. One grimoire, the *Grimorium Verum*, directed the sorcerer to stay away from all people beforehand, not just women, and another recommended that he avoid working and say a certain prayer—to God—once a day and twice a night for nine days before the ceremony. For the last few days, he was supposed to exist on a diet of bread and water.

Even the way a sorcerer bathed was important in most grimoires. The sorcerer was told to wash himself carefully in exorcised water (water from which all demons and evil spirits had been driven). His clothes—which some grimoires said should look like a clergyman's robes—must be spotless. Magic words had to be embroidered on them for some rituals. *The Key of Solomon* required that the sorcerer's clothes be woven of pure linen thread spun by a young virgin.

The equipment used in the rituals was to be just as carefully prepared. Brand-new candles must be used, said *The Key of Solo-*

mon. Wax images, if required, had to be blessed with holy water (holy water is exorcised and blessed water). The purest of parchment must be used for writing down the magic names and symbols, or for recording any pact that was made. True parchment is made from an animal's skin, usually a sheep's or a goat's. To ensure that it was pure, sorcerers often killed a kid and made their own. Outsiders viewed this as a sacrifice; some even said the kid was being sacrificed to the Devil; but most sorcerers denied this, claiming they killed only to ensure the purity of the skin.

There were elaborate instructions in some grimoires for how to kill the kid and make the parchment. There were also elaborate instructions for how to make the pen and ink with which to write on it. The pen, said the *Grimorium Verum,* should be made from a brand-new quill. It must be asperged (in this case, sprinkled with salted spring water shaken from a bundle of herbs) and "fumigated" with heated perfume. While the sorcerer was making the pen, he was to say: "Ababaloy, Samoy, Escavor, Adonay: I have expelled all illusion from this pen, that it may retain efficaciously within it the virtue necessary for all things which are used in the Art, as well for operations as for characters and conjurations. Amen." The inkwell was supposed to have various names for God written on it (including Eloym or Elohim), and the ink that went into it had to be exorcised and blessed, asperged, and fumigated, as did everything else that was used in the ceremony.

The ink could be made in various ways. For pacts, the sorcerer's blood had to be used for the signature, but the ink for the contract itself could be made from river water and a powder made out of gallnuts, Roman vitriol or green copperas, and rock alum or gum arabic. This mixture was boiled in an earthenware pot (a new one) over a fire made of vines cut at the March full moon and ferns picked on St. John's Eve. (St. John's Eve is June 21, so obviously one had to plan ahead!) Inks used for writing magic symbols had to be as carefully prepared.

Homemade knives or swords were important tools in many goetic rituals. An all-purpose knife could be made from new steel, heated and shaped, and then cooled in mole's blood (or gosling's blood). This blade was set into a white wooden handle with magic symbols carved on it. To frighten demons, however, one was better off with a black-handled knife, made in a similar way.

Which demons a sorcerer called depended on what he wanted to accomplish and which grimoire he was using. Although one thirteenth century sorcerer reportedly managed to raise Satan—inside a boot, no less—it was considered very risky to call on the original heavenly rebel. Another demon usually did just as well.

Let's say you're a sorcerer, using the *Grand Grimoire*, and you want to call the Grand Duke of Hell, Astaroth. Why Astaroth, especially since he smells so bad? Mostly because you probably live in the United States or Canada and, according to this grimoire, Astaroth commands two lieutenants, Sargatanus and Nebiros, who operate in North America.

To call Astaroth, you first have to know his seal and the sign he

Astaroth's seal and sign

makes himself known by (see page 103). You must write these characters on your parchment either in your own blood or in a sea tortoise's blood, or carve them on a ruby or on an emerald. Unless you carry or wear his seal and sign in one of these forms, Astaroth will not appear no matter what else you do.

Be prepared, when Astaroth does come, for his smell and for an apparition of any shape or size. If you're lucky, he'll appear as a black and white donkey or as a human being or even as an angel, but you should be ready for anything. If he comes as an angel he will probably be riding a dragon, and he will undoubtedly be carrying a poisonous snake. A magic ring, if you hold it in front of your face, *may* shield you from his smell.

Astaroth

Do you want to become invisible in order to hear what people say when they don't know you're around? Astaroth's lieutenant Sargatanus could help you, but *The Lesser Key of Solomon* or *Lemegeton* would suggest that you call Baal—if you're not afraid of his three heads and hoarse voice. Are you sick and in need of a fast cure? Try Marbas, then, the hellish president who will appear to you at first as a roaring lion—but, if you command him carefully, he will soon take on human shape and make you well again. Had a fight with your best friend? Amon, who holds the rank of marquis, might be able to help you patch it up. But stand back when he comes (being careful not to leave the circle), for Amon appears as a fierce snake-headed wolf with huge teeth, spitting fire. He, too, will assume human shape if you ask him to—but watch out for his teeth, for they will remain huge and dangerous. Is it love you want? You could try Beleth; his approach will be announced by musicians, but he himself will come thundering angrily to your circle on horseback. Draw your circle with a hazel wand if you plan to call Beleth, and be sure to wear a silver ring. Treat Beleth politely, too, or he will be terrible in his fury.

Okay, let's say you've reviewed all your preparations and you know which demon you want. Now you have to find out from your grimoire what day and what hour would be best for your ceremony, for most demons can only be "bound" during certain times. The *Lemegeton*, a good grimoire in which to look this up, will tell you that Solomon warns against summoning any demon at all on the second, fourth, sixth, ninth, tenth, twelfth, or fourteenth day of the moon. Astaroth, you will learn, can be called only on sunny days and only in the morning between sunrise and noon. Baal can be called between 9 A.M. and noon; Amon between 3 P.M. and 9 P.M.; Marbas at any time from sunrise to twilight. Each rank of demons has its proper time, and a great many of them, contrary to what many people think, must be called only during the day.

When the right day and time come, and you've fasted and bathed and made your parchment and knife, be sure you also make ready any special equipment you need for calling the particular demon you want. Draw your protective circle on the ground or on the floor with the greatest care, for it may be the only thing between you and disaster or death. Then draw a triangle around the circle. This is where the demon will stand while you remain in the circle; it symbolizes the triangle Solomon drew to contain the demons he bottled and threw in the well. Then on your parchment draw Solomon's seal (which looks like and probably is the forerunner of the Star of David). Also draw Solomon's pentagram. You should use rooster's blood for both these signs and also for the last one: the secret seal of Solomon. Then when all is ready, wash, put on a clean white linen robe (praying while you dress), and start your invocation, using the words the grimoire gives for calling the demon you have chosen.

He or she (but almost all are male) may not come the first time. In fact, it is likely that he will not. Never fear; the *Lemegeton* gives

Solomon's seal, pentagram, and secret seal

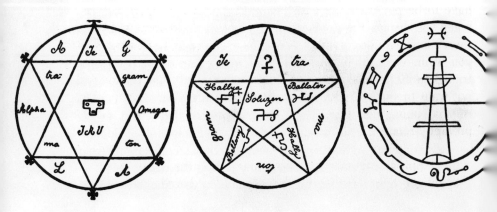

several invocations you can use. If none of them works, you must try to call your demon through his king. Let's say the demon you want is ruled by Amaymon, King of the East. You must say:

> O thou great and powerful King Amaymon, who rulest by the power of the Supreme God, El, over all Spirits, superior and inferior, but especially over the Infernal Order in the Dominion of the East, I invoke and command thee by the particular and true Name of God, and by the God whom thou dost worship, by the Seal of thy creation, by the most mighty and powerful Name of God, Jehovah, Tetragrammaton, who cast thee out of Heaven with the rest of the Infernal Spirits. . . . Do thou force and compel the Spirit [say the demon's name] here before this circle, in a fair and comely shape, without injury to myself or to any creature, that he may give me true and faithful answer, so that I may accomplish my desired end, whatsoever it be, provided that it is proper to his office, by the Power of God. . . .

When your demon comes, even if he or she has given you a hard time, it's important for you to be respectful as well as firm. You may have to be patient for a while longer to get full cooperation, but when you display the pentagram of Solomon, the demon will know there is no avoiding your wishes. When you're at last asked what you want, you will be able to "bind" your demon to stay in the triangle until he or she has done what you request. The demon will not want to stay long, so will probably give you your wish quickly. At that point, you should not let the demon linger, but should promptly recite this dismissal:

> O Spirit [say the demon's name], because thou hast diligently answered my demands, I do hereby license

thee to depart, without injury to man or beast. Depart, I say, and be thou very willing and ready to come, whensoever duly exorcised and conjured by the Sacred rites of Magic. I conjure thee to withdraw peaceably and quietly, and may the peace of God continue for ever between me and thee. Amen.

If you're lucky, your demon will leave with a minimum of fuss, and you can breathe a sigh of relief and enjoy whatever he or she has given you—unless, of course, like Devil's gold, it turns to toads!

8
The Devil's Minions: Pact Makers and Witches

IN THE SIXTH CENTURY in Cilicia, Asia Minor, there lived a good and pious priest named Theophilus, who put in many years of faithful service as a bishop's assistant. When the bishop died, it was suggested that Theophilus be made bishop in his place, but the humble priest refused, saying that he was not good enough. And so another man was installed as bishop, and Theophilus stayed on as his assistant.

It was not long before the new bishop learned that he had not been the first choice for the job and, what seemed worse, that his humble helper Theophilus had been the popular choice. Angrily, he had Theophilus removed from his job.

Theophilus was so hurt that he secretly went to a sorcerer and begged him to conjure up the Devil—Satan himself—so he could make a pact with him to get his job back.

The sorcerer agreed, and Satan appeared promptly to discuss the terms of the pact with Theophilus. Theophilus wanted his job; the Devil, as he always did in pacts, wanted Theophilus' soul and a statement that he would renounce his religion. The delivery date—when Theophilus would have to give up his soul—was seven years from the night the pact was made. All these terms were written on a piece of parchment which the Devil ordered Theophilus to sign (no doubt in blood) and seal.

Satan works quickly; that's one reason why so many people made pacts with him. The very next day, Theophilus got his job back. He soon became a rich man, able to afford luxuries and pleasures he had never known before. For seven years he was happy—but toward the end of that time, Theophilus began to feel nervous about dying and giving up his soul to the Devil. The frightened priest returned to the religion he had secretly renounced. After he had fasted and prayed to the Virgin Mary for forty days and nights, the statue of Mary in his church came down from its stand and comforted him. Her Son, she told Theophilus, had agreed he could be saved. The very next day Theophilus woke to find the contract lying on his chest. Overjoyed, he burned it to ashes. A few days later, after confessing his sins and telling the whole amazing story to his congregation, Theophilus died peacefully.

This story, which was one of the first of its kind, became the basis for many similar stories about Devil pacts. Without divine intervention, few pact makers were able to avoid giving up their souls when the time limit of the pact had expired. Not so with sorcerers; sorcerers could usually get out of it.

The *Grand Grimoire* is just about the only grimoire that speaks specifically of making a pact with a demon. This involves, of course, a complicated ritual. The sorcerer, says the *Grand Grimoire*, needs a newly cut hazel wand, a special stone, and two candles. He should go to a deserted place and draw a triangle with the stone, put the candles on each side of the triangle, and write the name of Jesus under it. Then he must stand in the middle of the triangle, holding the hazel rod, his grimoire, and the pact, already written on parchment and signed in blood. The pact should say that he will "reward" the demon in twenty years if the demon will lead him to treasure.

But most pacts made like this were tricks, because the sorcerer usually had no intention of fulfilling his part of the bargain. The usual reaction of a demon to a sorcerer's desire to make a pact was to agree—on the condition that the sorcerer surrender his body and soul in twenty years. But the sorcerer would seldom promise to do this. He'd just hand the demon the signed pact—which of course only said the demon would be "rewarded"; it never said in what way. At the most, a sorcerer might pay the demon "one coin on the first Monday of each month" and agree to summon him only once a week between 10 P.M. and 2 A.M. Most demons, under these circumstances, probably considered themselves very lucky if even those mild terms were fulfilled.

Occasionally, a sorcerer did make a more binding pact, one in which he actually stated he would give up his soul and body. But, even if he was that rash, he could usually get out of it by begging God's forgiveness—or simply by spitting three times. The most famous sorcerer who ever escaped a pact, however, did so not by his own efforts but because a woman interceded for him. But even he, a German sorcerer named Faust, didn't get out of the pact in all versions of his story. Faust, or Dr. Faustus, was a real person whose story became a legend. Each time it was retold, the details changed a little.

The real Faust lived in Germany in the beginning of the sixteenth century. Although literary versions of his story made him into a great scholar, he was really a cheap magician and a not very good doctor who traveled around like a strolling player. He had studied magic on the side while studying medicine legitimately. Wherever he went, Faust boasted about what a clever sorcerer and necromancer he was. He was such a braggart that few people believed he could do half of what he claimed. They called him a "pretender to magic," and more than once he was asked to leave a town where he tried to "practice."

But the stories about his powers persisted nonetheless. People said his assistant, his black dog, and his horse were demons. And when he died—he was, it seems, killed violently—the rumor immediately started that the Devil had claimed his soul.

Because the real Faust had been suspected of dealing with the Devil, it was not long before books of magic were attributed to him as they had been to Solomon—and with about as much justification; it is unlikely that Faust wrote any of them. More famous were books and stories written about Faust. The first one appeared in 1587 and was called the *History of Dr. Johann Faust.* In it, Faust summoned a devil named Mephistopheles (probably Satan) and made a twenty-four-year pact with him. Many writers were impressed by the dramatic possibilities of this tale, among them the English playwright Christopher Marlowe, who wrote a play called *The Tragical History of the Life and Death of Doctor Faustus.* One legend says that the Devil himself appeared at one performance!

In Marlowe's play, Faust is a great scholar longing for knowledge. Throughout the play, he regrets that he has made a Devil pact, even though Mephistopheles shows him all kinds of wonders and gives him everything he wants. In the end, Faust begs God to take his soul. But it is too late, and when he dies, he is carried off to hell by devils.

In what is probably the most famous version of the story, however, Faust is saved. In the play *Faust*, written by the eighteenth-century German poet Johann Wolfgang von Goethe, our hero is also a great scholar. He longs to know the real world as well as he knows the world of books. With the help of *The Key of Solomon* he makes Mephistopheles appear and draws up a pact with him. For years—without the whiny regrets expressed by Marlowe's Faust—he wanders the earth gathering worldly knowledge and experience. Still, it looks as if his soul must go to Mephistopheles when he dies. It does not; Gretchen, a woman whom he once loved and who has long

Faust performing magic in his study. Engraving by Rembrandt Harmensz van Rijn.

The Tragicall Hiftorie of the Life and Death of Doctor Fauftus.

With new Additions.

Written by C H. M A R.

Printed at London for *Iohn Wright*, and are to be fold at his fhop without Newgate. 1631.

Title page from an old edition of Marlowe's Doctor Faustus.

since died, pleads his case in heaven, and at the last minute the pact is dissolved and Faust's soul is saved.

Ordinary people, though, rarely had that kind of luck. It is true, at least according to an old English ballad, that one humble man's wife saved him from the Devil—but that was because the pact said the man wouldn't have to deliver his soul if he could show the Devil an animal he'd never seen before. The man's clever wife covered herself with feathers and pretended her rear end was her head. The Devil fell for it, and the man's soul was saved. That kind of thing, however, was rare. Most pacts ended, like William Gruff's, in death:

Gruff, a former pirate, lived outside of Baltimore, Maryland, in the late 1700s. He was so unfriendly people called him Surly Bill, and no one spoke to him unless they absolutely had to. That probably suited Surly Bill fine, for his one aim in life was to be rich, and for some time, he'd been trying to raise the Devil in order to ask him for help. Night after night, Bill mixed up noxious brews in an iron caldron and muttered various spells over them. But nothing happened—till the night he got a letter from the Devil.

Had you been able to read over Bill's shoulder, you would have seen that the letter contained a few lines only, but they were directions for completing the Devil-raising spell. Blood was the missing ingredient, said the letter. Then it instructed Bill to go to the Forest Ring the next night at midnight.

The Forest Ring was a clearing in deep woods not far from where Bill lived. The next night, when the moon was full and no creature was about, Bill ran there from his cabin. Breathlessly, he burst out of the woods and into the clearing, expecting to see the Archfiend with all his demons—but he saw nothing at all except the moonlight on the grass and the dark surrounding trees.

When he looked again he saw a stump, and leaning against the stump he saw a gun, and under the gun was another letter from guess who. This one told him that the blood he needed to finish his spell had to be the blood of a murderer, and that the gun was his to get it with. Clever Devil—that way, he would get two souls: the murderer's first and, later, Bill's.

It didn't take Bill long to choose his victim. Back in his pirate days he'd made his share of enemies. It was easy to decide on the bitterest of these, the murderer Captain Jack Reefer.

Within a few weeks Bill had found Captain Jack, killed him, collected his blood in a bottle, and returned home. For three nights he poured some of the precious murderer's blood into the brew in his caldron. It was not until the third night that anything happened. On that night, a tremendous storm blew up and at its peak, in a great flash of lightning, the Devil himself appeared before Surly Bill.

As the Devil stepped toward him, his gimlet eyes relentlessly boring into Bill's, Bill cried out in terror and would have given anything to undo what he had done. But it was too late. Grasping Bill's arm with a steely grip, the Devil made his deal: "I will serve you for five years and give you all the money you can spend. But five years from this night you will return to the Forest Ring from wherever in the world you are, and you will be mine." With his clawlike finger, the Devil made his mark on Bill's forehead and vanished.

For five years Bill traveled throughout the world, wearing fine clothes and drinking and gambling to his heart's content. Whenever Bill drank too much, the Devil's mark on his forehead turned bright red, frightening away his companions and reminding Bill of the fate that was in store for him. As the time approached, he decided on a plan: he would simply go as far away from Maryland as he could, and he would not return, no matter what.

But his plan was doomed. Although Bill was thousands of miles from the Forest Ring when he was due to return to keep his date with the Devil, he felt himself drawn irresistibly back home. No matter what he did, he could not ignore the mysterious pull; he had to obey it.

And so, exactly five years from the night the Devil had marked him, Surly Bill stood once more in the Forest Ring in a circle of demons while a huge storm raged. Lightning split the sky, and the greatest devil of all strode to Bill's side. . . .

The next morning when the storm had spent its force and all was calm, the sun rose on the body of William Gruff, lying in the middle of the Forest Ring—stone-cold dead.

It is hard to imagine that anyone was worse off than Surly Bill, but witches probably were—especially those people who, in the days of the Inquisition, were accused in court of having made Devil pacts. Witches, it was believed, did not summon the Devil as sorcerers did. They were the Devil's servants rather than his masters. Consequently, their contracts were different from those made by sorcerers or even by ordinary people like Bill.

The terms of witch-Devil pacts were extremely humble. The witches rarely if ever got great wealth in return for their souls; they were more likely to be assured of enough food to keep from starving, help in time of trouble, and the right to be entertained at their sabbats (worship services). In return they had to agree to renounce Christianity and do the Devil's bidding at all times. That often meant bringing him babies as sacrifices or bringing him converts—new witches to serve him.

Satan marking one of his followers.

Contracts between witches and the Devil were rarely written down and were usually "signed" by the witch's kissing the Devil's rear end during his or her initiation. The Devil would then mark the witch with his claw, usually in a more hidden place than the forehead, where Surly Bill was marked. Witch contracts, written or not, were usually for the duration of the witch's life; the Devil, of course, wouldn't want to shorten the life of someone who was serving him. Even when, as occasionally happened, the contract was for a certain number of years, it was usually renewed when the stated time was up.

Well, maybe. Those are some of the things the Inquisitors said about witch contracts when they were looking for witches to burn. No one, however, has ever proved that such contracts were actually made—or any others for that matter. As for the witches themselves, many scholars think that most of the people burned during the Inquisition for practicing witchcraft were innocent of any kind of relationship with the Devil, except whatever existed in their own or the Inquisitors' imaginations.

9
Devil Worship and Satanism

NO ONE KNOWS FOR SURE whom the old-time witches really worshiped, although modern witches and many scholars say that the small number of people who really were witches probably worshiped ancient pagan gods. During the days of the Inquisition, however, Church authorities and most other people were sure that witches worshiped the Devil. Records of witch trials held during that period are full of lurid descriptions of how they did it.

Although the details varied from trial to trial and place to place, the typical witches' sabbat supposedly took place on a night with a full moon, especially at the time of a pagan feast like Samhain (Halloween), Midsummer, or May Eve. On such a night, in quiet villages and lonely peasant cottages, witches, mostly women, would creep out of their beds, leaving a transformed broomstick or footstool behind as a stand-in to fool their families. Silently they would anoint their bodies with "flying ointment" and, mounting their familiars—or extra broomsticks—would fly off through the night, bound for a lonely clearing deep within a forest to meet and worship and celebrate with other witches.

The order of events is not always clear from the trial records, but at most sabbats, according to testimony which was often gotten by means of torture, there was apparently some kind of worship service. This service usually centered around a goatlike figure who was said by some to be the devil himself and by others to be a demon or even a witch representing him. He was usually addressed as "Grand Master" and frequently was the head of the coven, or group of witches, gathered in the clearing. (The number of witches in a coven has always varied, although thirteen is sometimes considered the ideal number.)

As part of the ceremony—according to testimony during the Inquisition—new witches were initiated into the group. They agreed to serve the Devil and received their familiars from him. Then they were marked by his claw (sometimes by his tooth). Established witches renewed their pledge to serve their master, and sometimes reported on their activities since the last Sabbat. Then

The Devil presiding over a sabbat feast.

there was usually a huge celebration, loud and raucous and often obscene—again, according to trial testimony during the Inquisition. A meal was served, sometimes delicious, but, according to some people accused of being witches, sometimes horrible. Wine flowed freely and the witches danced, usually either back to back or "widdershins"—to the left; both were considered improper. Sometimes there was also an orgy.

The most offensive part of the sabbat, to Church officials especially, was the worship service. Most people were sure it was a mock Catholic Mass in which most everything was the reverse of what it is in a normal Catholic service. Prayers, for example, were supposedly said backward, and the name of Satan was used instead of the name of God or Christ. Instead of holy water, the water used in the Black Mass, as this ceremony was called, was stagnant and foul-smelling; sometimes blood was used. Instead of wearing white robes, the Grand Master wore black. Black candles were burned instead of white, and the Host, or communion wafer, round in Catholic Masses, was triangular. Sometimes it was black or red in color.

But many people doubt that the Black Mass in any form was a normal part of a witches' sabbat. Certainly it was not if the witches worshiped pagan gods, although if they did and people spied on them, the spies may have *thought* they were seeing a parody of the Mass.

Witches were not the only people who were accused of holding Black Masses. The accusation was leveled against almost all heretical groups. Many people accused of heresy as well as people accused of being witches confessed under torture to Devil worship of some kind. It didn't matter much to the Inquisitors, apparently, that many of the accused took back their confessions once the pain had stopped.

It's hard to say, then, what really went on in private worship services in those days and what gruesome details were invented by

Church officials in order to force people to worship the way the Inquisition wanted them to. A good example of just how hard the truth was to find is the story of the Knights Templar, a group founded in the early twelfth century after the Crusaders had captured Jerusalem.

The purpose of this group of religious military men from various nations was to keep watch over Jerusalem, making sure that Christian visitors were not harmed and that the city itself stayed in Christian hands. At first, their cause was a very popular one, and their order attracted members from many countries. Many Templars were rich noblemen who turned over most of their land and riches to the order. This made the order itself wealthy and soon the Templars were so rich they could loan money to national governments. It was not long before they controlled European finance, and this made them so powerful that governments saw them as a threat to their own power—especially the government of France, in whose country the Templars had their headquarters and their treasury.

As the Templars' power grew, their popularity diminished. Various popes granted them increasing privileges and eventually they were even allowed to ignore papal orders addressed to the religious community as a whole unless they were specifically told not to. Their members could not be excommunicated—barred from the Church—by either priests or bishops. That meant, in effect, that the Templars could not be punished (except by the pope) for being heretics—and that is exactly what people now suspected them of being. It was certainly true that the members of the order were very closemouthed about their religious ceremonies. Soon people whispered that the Templars performed odd secret rituals in the dead of night—goetic rituals, perhaps. Maybe they even worshiped the Devil!

While these dark rumors spread, King Philip IV of France tried to limit the Templars' power. He wasn't very successful, though, because his own government was so poverty-stricken that he had to borrow heavily from the Templars' treasury. In 1307, Philip had many leading Templars arrested. These men were tortured and many died—but not before admitting to blasphemous religious practices similar to those that people had been whispering about.

Philip requested that the pope, Clement V, look into the possibility that the Templars were performing horrible satanic rites. By November, the pope had issued orders for the arrest of Templars all over Europe. Trials and executions followed. It was not long before the pope declared that the Templars were "apostates [people who desert their original religion] and impure" and forbade anyone to protect them. Then, in 1312, he officially dissolved the order as being heretical.

Meanwhile, the confessions had been pouring in—confessions made under torture. Individual Templars admitted that they forced new members of their order to denounce Jesus, Mary, and God and spit on or trample the cross; they admitted that they let laymen forgive people for their sins—something only priests were officially allowed to do. Some admitted to kneeling before a human head—or a cat or a golden calf—instead of before God. The head, some said, was the head of their first Grand Master, or leader. Others said it was Baphomet, a goatish-looking deity who supposedly was an Arabian god or demon—or perhaps even a form of Mohammed, prophet of Islam, the very religion the Templars were supposed to be fighting. The exact nature of what individual Templars confessed to worshiping didn't matter much in the long run. Obviously whatever it was, it wasn't God; therefore it must be the Devil—and their accusers went on from there, often extravagantly: demons worked as familiars to the Templars; the Devil claimed one Templar's soul a year; the Templars used unconsecrated Hosts at Mass; they wore charms dedicated to their "head"; they murdered children, sometimes their own, and then burned them to make magic powder from the ashes; they summoned the Devil to appear at their ceremonies; they held orgies. Soon almost every horrible or weird

Baphomet, whom the Templars were accused of worshiping.

thing anyone could think of was being attributed to the Templars.

There were so many political maneuvers against the Templars it is almost impossible to say whether any of the charges against them were true. Some of their defenders said they asked new members to commit blasphemous acts as a test—that since their job was to protect Jerusalem, the Templars had to see how new members would react under pressure from their enemies if they were captured. Others said it was true that the Templars treated the cross with disrespect, but that they did so because it had caused pain to Christ. There have been similar explanations for other things the Templars were accused of doing. We will never fully know their side of the story—for during the Templars' trials in Paris, the Court refused to hear 573 people who stood ready to testify on their behalf.

Everyone knew, though, what the Templars' own Grand Master said. Jacques de Molay confessed to all kinds of heresy when he was first arrested. But later he took back his words and loudly proclaimed his and the order's innocence; another Templar leader, Gaufrid de Charnay, backed him up. The two men made their statement before a huge Paris crowd in March 1314—a crowd which had gathered to hear them admit to their heresies, beg forgiveness, and be accepted with pardon back into the Church—and then be led away to life imprisonment. None of that happened, though. As soon as Philip heard about the men's public retraction, he ordered their immediate execution.

Although the Templars provided the biggest Devil-worship scandal of their era, there were others. The Freemasons, for example, an organization which is still in existence, was thought to be a Devil-worshiping sect. Although this building crafts guild practiced rites that had some religious significance, no one has ever been able to find any evidence that their rites involved Devil worship.

Even so, one cannot say, "There is no such thing as Devil worship." There is and perhaps there almost always has been. In a way, Devil worship goes back to the days when people worshiped "evil" gods to make sure those gods would not harm them, and it continued right on into those times when people admired Satan because he seemed more exciting or more human than God. At that point, however, Devil worship tended to become Satanism. There's a difference, although perhaps a subtle one. A Devil worshiper bowed down before the Devil in total humility. He or she was completely in the Devil's control, as witches were said to be during the Inquisition. A true Satanist—at least according to some Satanists of today—was no abject worshiper. Satan was seen by Satanists essentially as an equal, and as an embodiment of freedom and sensuality who could help them find self-fulfillment. He was neither their master, as he was to the more humble Devil worshipers—nor their servant, as he and other demons were to sorcerers.

Even so, Satanism has ranged in practice from a religion dedicated to self-fulfillment to a cult devoted to evil. One of the most bizarre Satanic rituals, the Black Mass, pretty much covered the whole range, depending on how it was celebrated. Certainly when babies or children were sacrificed as part of the Mass, it was evil, but when the most out-of-the-way thing that happened was that a naked woman or a coffin served as the altar—well, it might be strange, but it certainly wasn't anywhere near as evil as doing murder.

By the fifteenth century, the main examples of simple Devil worship came from the witches' sabbats told about in the Inquisition's trials. But during that period there was also at least one horrifying Satanism case. This was the case against Gilles de Rais, a former comrade of Joan of Arc. In 1440, Gilles de Rais was executed for murdering somewhere between two hundred and eight hundred children, most of them boys. He was accused of using their blood in satanic ceremonies. With the blood of his first victim, goes one story, de Rais—who may have been the basis for the fictional character Bluebeard—wrote and signed a Devil pact. From then on he sacrificed children to Satan in elaborate Black Masses performed at regular intervals in his lavish castle. It was said at his trial that he hired sorcerers to raise demons, among them Belial, Beelzebub, and even Satan himself. Again, no one can be sure how much of this was fact and how much was fiction. Certainly de Rais was a sick man who probably did murder children. But no one knows whether he really practiced Satanism or whether his crimes were so horrible that people just thought he did.

Even though many people accused of being witches admitted to participating in Black Masses, some scholars think that there was no real Black Mass outside of people's imaginations until one was "written" by Catherine de Médicis, wife of Henry II of France, in the sixteenth century. After Henry died, so the story goes, Catherine, who had always been intrigued by the occult, worked out a ceremony with some friends in which the Catholic Mass was read backward and the altar was a naked girl. This bizarre ceremony—without any malevolent purpose—soon became an upper-class fad and even spread to other countries. A century later, Madame de Montespan, jealous mistress of King Louis XIV of France, was taking part in similar ceremonies, but not for the fun of it. Madame de Montespan at first held Amatory Masses to make Louis stay in love with her. When those didn't work, she had Mortuary Masses performed in order to kill him. At those, supposedly, infants were sacrificed and Asmodeus, Astaroth, and Lucifer were summoned. They didn't work any better than the other Masses, however, and Madame de Montespan ended her days in exile.

Fashionable Satanism, of the kind supposedly practiced by Catherine de Médicis, reached its peak in the eighteenth century, when people seemed especially fascinated by the descriptions of the Black Mass that had come out of the Inquisition. People even formed clubs devoted to the Black Mass and to Satanism. The most famous of these was the Hell Fire Club in England, founded by the wealthy Sir Francis Dashwood and a couple of his friends. The club's meeting place was a ruined but renovated abbey. The inscription over the door read *"Fay ce que voudras,"* which means "Do whatever you want." That, apparently, is exactly what Sir Francis and his friends did until they got bored and disbanded.

For a while after that Satanism declined as a fad. But enough Black Masses were still celebrated, it seems, to prompt a man named Eugene Vintras to form a group which celebrated "White Masses" for people who felt threatened by Black Masses! Then in 1891 a book was published which revived people's interest in Satanism as a decadent fad. The book, called *La Bas*, was written by a man named J. K. Huysmans, who said he had attended a Black Mass and therefore knew what he was talking about in the scene in which he described one. He had also done a lot of research on the subject, and had even gotten some of his information from a leader of the White Mass group.

When Huysmans' book was still popular, one hundred Hosts were stolen from the Cathedral of Notre Dame in Paris. Hosts were also stolen from churches elsewhere in France. People began wondering if there was an upsurge of Satanism; priests started locking the boxes in which the Hosts were kept. A suspicious-looking chapel was found in Rome—a chapel with black candles at its altar, heavy black and red drapes, and a huge tapestry of the Devil on one wall. Huysmans and others made extravagant claims for a widespread network of Satanists. But most of this "authoritative" information—including a juicy bit of gossip saying that a satanic pope had his headquarters in Charleston, South Carolina—turned out to be someone's idea of an elaborate practical joke.

At about this same time in England a man who was to become one of the best-known satanic figures of the twentieth century was beginning to develop his interest in the occult. He was "the Great Beast"—Aleister Crowley, "the Wickedest Man in the World."

Crowley was a self-styled magician, a bit like the real Faust, but fancier. Had he lived in Faust's time, he almost certainly would have been suspected of making a pact with the Devil, for he, like Faust, made outrageous claims about his evil deeds. But since Crowley lived in a time when Satanism was more "in" than pact making, he was thought of as a Satanist. Apparently, he lapped it up eagerly. The more evil people thought he was, the better he liked it.

Crowley had started out with a fairly harmless interest in the occult. In 1898 he joined the well-known and respectable English occult society called the Hermetic Order of the Golden Dawn. No one could find fault with that; in fact, one of its members was the famous Irish poet William Butler Yeats.

But eventually, after quarreling with some of the Hermetic Order's members, Crowley began doing bizarre things like shaving his head, trying to raise demons, practicing magic, and taking heroin. After a long trip, during which people from Egypt to the

Aleister Crowley

United States were able to observe his antics, Crowley set himself up in Cefalù, Sicily, in a villa which he called the Abbey of Thelema. There he dedicated himself, or so he said, to evil. For a while no one cared much what went on within the walls of the Abbey, but eventually the rumors began: Crowley's ceremonies were getting dangerously bloody, people said; he had sacrificed a baby in one of his rituals, and someone associated with him had died mysteriously. That was enough for Crowley's neighbors; he was forced to return to his native England.

There had already been rumors about Crowley when he was in the United States. People thought, for example, that he had founded satanic temples, and that he himself was a confirmed Satanist. But no one was actually sure, and people still argue about it today. Some say that Crowley wasn't a Satanist at all, or even an exclusively goetic magician, that he was simply someone who experimented with all kinds of magic; naturally he'd run into demons at some point if he did that.

When he died in 1947, Crowley (whose last comment supposedly was a rather pathetic, "I am perplexed") left behind a lot of stories, essays, and other writings about his ideas. These, along with the strange deeds he is supposed to have done, have influenced modern ideas about Satanism. But only some modern Satanists think of Crowley as the evil sorcerer he said he was. Many, like most modern witches, refuse to accept "the Great Beast" as one of their own.

No one is too sure exactly how many Satanists there are today in the United States, but some estimates put the figure as high as one hundred thousand. In type, they cover the whole range, from satanic groups who deal in brutality and murder to relatively harmless ones who think of Satan as a god of pleasure and the happy life. The California group called the First Church of Satan, for example, doesn't seem to be particularly destructive. Founded in 1966, this organization, which claims to have seven thousand members in various parts of the world, is of the "Satanism is doing whatever you want to do" school of thought. They use some of the trappings of grimmer satanic rites—the naked-female or coffin altar, for example—but they are not, they say, either Devil worshipers or evil worshipers. Instead, they say, they are devoted to pleasure and personal fulfillment.

Other modern satanic groups, however, do appear to be devoted to evil. Even in the 1970s, there have been reports of Satanists who have committed murder. In 1972, for example, one Illinois group supposedly performed sacrifices. In Vineland, New Jersey, a young Satanist asked his friends to help him kill himself, for he believed that after his death he would be able to return to earth leading a group of demons. In 1973 a New Jersey girl testified in court that she was a satanic priestess and that she had witnessed the sacrificial killing of a California boy. Best-known supposed Satanist of the 1970s is Charles Manson, who was convicted in 1971 of the murder of movie starlet Sharon Tate and six other people. But although Manson was widely believed to have been the leader of a satanic group, no one really ever proved it.

What, then, is a modern Satanist? Is a person a Satanist just because he or she does bizarre or cruel things to which people attach the label "Satanism"? Is a person a Satanist just because he or she says, "I'm a Satanist"?

Only one thing seems certain. Those people who actually have practiced rituals involving "sacrificial" killings are criminals and are suffering from severe psychological problems—no matter what they call themselves or are called by others. The label "Satanist" may make it easier for these people to cope with their problems, but it doesn't change the fact that what they have done is cruel and against the law.

As for the other Satanist groups—well, those which, like the First Church of Satan, apparently do nothing criminal or harmful to others, do seem to have strong ties to those Satanists of long ago who admired Satan as an independent, rebellious, and pleasure-loving spirit. Perhaps they have a somewhat better claim to the label "Satanist."

10
Possession and Exorcism

WILLIAM PETER BLATTY's popular book *The Exorcist*, made into an equally popular movie released in 1973, was not a true story, but it was based on one. In January 1949, a fourteen-year-old Washington, D. C., boy, Douglass Deen, first startled and then frightened his family by showing distinct signs of being possessed—of having demons inside his body who controlled his actions.

Douglass' problem started as a fairly simple case of poltergeist haunting. A poltergeist or "mischievous ghost" is, according to occultists, a spirit which usually attaches itself to a house in which there are teenagers or people close to their teens. It then makes a general nuisance of itself, hurling dishes and furniture around, throwing rocks, and making weird noises at night. Poltergeists used to be thought of as demons, and some early cases of possession, especially in the 1600s, began just as Douglass' did. Poltergeists can be more than annoying, since they prevent people from sleeping and frighten them badly, but in more recent times they have not generally been believed to be anywhere near as deeply evil as demons.

The Deens, then, in the early days of Douglass' possession, were upset but not terrified. At first, they simply heard odd noises inside the walls of their house. That was easy enough to explain: mice, probably, or squirrels. But then furniture started moving when no one was around to touch it. That wasn't so easy to explain. Then the poltergeist—or whatever it was—shook Douglass' bed. One might think, of course, that the family was making this up to get attention, or that Douglass was, but at least one outsider, their minister, observed a bed shake while Douglass was in it. He also saw a chair in which Douglass was sitting tip over even though Douglass himself hadn't moved a muscle. The minister was convinced something supernatural was at work.

Eventually, when everyone was sure Douglass was possessed by a demon instead of just haunted by a simple poltergeist (or playing a practical joke), a Jesuit priest was called in to exorcise the demon—

A woman being exorcised. Note the demon leaving on the right, above her head.

throw it out. But every time the priest prayed, Douglass—or the demon inside him—swore angrily. Douglass' body shook uncontrollably; his voice was abnormally high, and once in a while he even spoke in Latin. That would have been fine—except Douglass didn't know any Latin. This state of affairs continued unchanged for some time. And then in May the demon—or whatever it was—left as quickly and unexplainably as it had arrived months earlier.

Douglass showed a few of the typical signs of possession. Regan, Blatty's heroine, showed even more. Here are some of the most typical ones, starting with Douglass':

· blind anger and swearing, especially when faced with prayers or religious objects, or when forced to go to church; blasphemy; being burned by holy water and repelled by the cross

· speaking or understanding a language one doesn't know

· having convulsions; shaking; going rigid; performing extraordinary feats of strength or seemingly impossible contortions; levitation (rising up in the air, often in a lying-down position)

· the ability to prophesy and read minds

· coldness, headaches, dizziness, pain, a noisy digestion; vomiting; vomiting strange objects; foaming at the mouth; sudden unexplained wounds; a swollen belly and a black, protruding tongue; fainting; trancelike states; bleeding though there is no wound; rolling one's eyes; smelling horrible; skin ailments; a change in appetite; an abnormally high pulse and respiration rate

· the sensation that something is eating away one's stomach; the sensation that something is burning or biting one's body

· loss of identity; not knowing when one is oneself and when one "is" the demon

As you can see, being possessed isn't a whole lot of fun!

One of the possession symptoms which has fascinated people most is the ability to speak or understand a language that one doesn't know. Strange though this seems, it has happened in case after case, and no one has been able to offer a really satisfactory explanation. The closest anyone has come, perhaps, is the explanation offered by some parapsychologists (those who study occult phenomena). They say that usually in such cases someone in the room, often the exorcist, knows the language the possessed person suddenly starts speaking; the possessed person, they say, has "learned" the language through some kind of mental telepathy. But this is an unproved theory, and so this symptom remains one of the least understood of all manifestations of possession. In fact, it is so strange that the sudden ability to speak or understand a foreign tongue is sometimes accepted, even today, as a sign that a person is truly possessed instead of a fraud or a victim of some kind of illness.

Another extraordinary possession symptom, and one which Blatty's heroine exhibited, is that of taking on the appearance of the demon doing the possessing, and speaking in his or her (usually his) voice. People who are possessed are said to look completely different from the way they ordinarily look and to speak in voices totally unlike their own. This is hard to believe, but it is certainly consistent with the theory behind possession: that the demon not only takes over the victim's body, but also replaces the victim's personality with his or her own.

Demonic possession is no respecter of persons, although there are records of more women than men being affected. More poor people than rich people have suffered from possession, more uneducated than educated people, and more bored and lonely people than people who were busy and fulfilled. Possession in convents was not at all unusual in the seventeenth century—a time when nuns rarely had jobs to do, as they often do today, and when convents themselves were apt to be damp, unhealthy places. One of the most famous possession cases of all time occurred in an Ursuline convent in Loudun, France.

The convent at Loudun was a small one, located in an old house people believed was haunted—that must have gotten things off to a running start! The trouble centered on the prioress, an ambitious young woman called Sister Jeanne des Anges. Sister Jeanne, people said, was secretly in love with a secular priest named Urbain Grandier (a secular priest was not bound by rules as strict as those binding regular priests).

Sister Jeanne wasn't the only woman in love with Grandier, secretly or otherwise. Since he'd come to Loudun in 1617, he'd already made many conquests—and as many enemies. One girl bore him a child, but he refused to marry her. This made him a powerful enemy, for the girl's father was the public prosecutor—sort of like the district attorney. He actually did marry another woman—or at least he convinced her that the secret ceremony he performed himself late one night in church was a proper wedding. If the woman was convinced, she was the only one who was; the ceremony caused, as one might imagine, quite a scandal when word of it leaked out.

All these and other shenanigans led to Grandier's arrest in 1629 for what amounted to "conduct unbecoming a priest," even a secular one. Though he eventually won his case and was set free, he had made a lot more enemies by then. They hadn't become any fewer by 1632, when the trouble started at the convent. It was then that poor Sister Jeanne began having fits.

Not long before her fits started, Sister Jeanne had asked Grandier to take the place of the nuns' spiritual adviser and personal priest, who had just died. After Grandier refused, Sister Jeanne began dreaming that he visited her at night. Then she and other nuns began seeing ghosts in the halls. Young girls, boarding at the convent and attending school there, had the covers pulled off them at night; girls and nuns heard mysterious moans.

After a while, when there was no letup in these strange goings-on, the nuns' confessor, Canon Mignon (who was related to the public prosecutor and was therefore not overfond of Grandier), offered his opinion. Privately, he was sure the trouble was caused by practical jokers, but he told the nuns that their tormentors were probably demons.

That was all the already agitated nuns needed. Soon both they and most people around them were convinced they were possessed. Worse than that, they were convinced that Grandier was the cause of their possession. How? Why, he had bewitched them, of course, by sending demons into their bodies to torment them!

Once this idea started spreading, chaos broke out. One after the other, the nuns began to exhibit all the classic signs of possession. Sister Jeanne was described by one visitor, Thomas Killigrew, as an attractive woman with black eyes and brown hair; but when she was in the middle of a fit, he said, her otherwise attractive face turned ugly—in fact, it usually resembled Asmodeus' face, or Zabulon's, two of the demons who she said possessed her. (The others were Leviathan, Isacaaron, Gresil, Behemoth, Haman, and Balaam.) Killigrew said that Sister Jeanne's eyes rolled back till you could see only the bloodshot whites, and her tongue, swollen and black, lolled out of her mouth. Occasionally, one of her demons would let her laugh normally. But during most of her fits, Sister Jeanne laughed horribly if she laughed at all, and rolled immodestly on the floor, moaning and swearing in a hoarse male voice.

The other sixteen nuns in the convent all showed similar symptoms. Some had swollen stomachs; some foamed at the mouth and beat themselves; some even tried to kiss priests. They were all pious and sweet and proper between fits, but when the fits came, they all turned rough and coarse and horrible.

Canon Mignon was their first exorcist, but the job was so difficult that he soon had to send for reinforcements. One of the first suggested that the exorcisms be made public. As a result, in October 1632, the possessed nuns of Loudun became big-time entertainment. It worked like this: When the crowd—sometimes as many as seven thousand people—had assembled, Sister Jeanne and the other nuns were led quietly in. With great solemnity, their exorcists would pray and order the demons to leave. At first, the nuns would keep their composure, but soon, almost as if their exorcists had given them the idea, they (or the demons within them) would burst into a loud string of swear words and foul, blasphemous language. The shocked spectators pressed forward to watch the nuns thrash around on the floor and see their stomachs swell and to keep track of the dramatic battle between demons and exorcists. And, although the good people of Loudun and nearby towns undoubtedly clucked their tongues in horror at what they saw, they kept coming back for more.

That October, Asmodeus was expelled from Sister Jeanne, leaving her, however, still with seven demons. Soon afterward some local officials came to see her. Her exorcists questioned her in their presence and she repeated, unmistakably, her charge against Grandier.

It was not until December 1633 that Grandier was arrested. Then he was searched for a Devil's mark. All suspicious-looking places on his body were pricked with a long needle, for Devil's marks, supposedly, were insensitive to pain. Sure enough, two insensitive spots were found on his body, "proving" that he was a witch and therefore, people thought, capable of sending demons into the nuns. True, a number of people in positions of authority thought it was a put-up job; they even doubted that the good sisters were truly possessed. But that didn't matter; Grandier had too many powerful enemies. Besides, the public exorcisms convinced most of the ordinary people of the truth of the accusations. So did some papers supposedly found in Grandier's house: a paper written by him saying that it was all right for priests to marry, and a pact, signed by Grandier and various demons, including Satan, Beelzebub, Leviathan, and Astaroth.

By spring, Grandier found himself awaiting trial in a prison made just for him—the attic of an ordinary house with bricks blocking the windows and iron bars covering the chimney. A bit of straw thrown on the floor was all Grandier had for a bed.

The pact that Grandier supposedly signed with Satan and other demons.

Oddly enough, during the period when Grandier appeared at pretrial hearings, things were fairly quiet at the convent. There were, in fact, no public exorcisms for several months. But as the August trial date approached, the nuns and their exorcists once again became public spectacles. By now their fame had spread far from Loudun. People from all over France and even some from other countries packed each "performance" and there were so many visitors that the little town's population had doubled by the time the trial opened. Some of the nuns, people whispered, had recently vomited pacts which showed once again that Grandier had bewitched them; surely the man was guilty, shockingly so!

Even before the trial opened it was obvious that Grandier didn't have a chance. By August 18 it was all over; he was sentenced not only to be burned alive at the stake (people were usually strangled first), but also to kneel outside two different churches in his nightshirt with a rope around his neck and ask pardon of both God and the king. Before that, his head, beard, body, and eyebrows were to be shaved. Someone wanted to pull out his fingernails too, but when the time came the doctor who shaved him refused.

It was to be a humiliating and painful death, but Grandier, whatever else he'd done in life, met it with dignity. He denied he had bewitched the nuns, and when he was asked to sign a confession, he refused, saying that he couldn't confess to something he hadn't done. So he was tortured, and by the time they were through with him he was so badly mangled he had to be carried in a cart to the churches where he was to ask for pardon. A priest at one church was so moved by his courage that he hugged him and said he would pray for him.

The place of execution was mobbed. Grandier was told he would have a chance to speak to the crowd, but he never did, because people kept shouting at him to confess. By the time they quieted down, it was too late; the fire had already been lit. A fly was seen diving into the flames; pigeons circled above them. The spectators were sure that they were demons, claiming Grandier's soul. Later, Sister Jeanne said the fly was his familiar.

That very night, though Grandier was dead, the nuns continued having fits and their exorcists went on praying over them and ordering the demons to leave. It was three more years before those demons were finally expelled. At least one of the exorcists died soon after Grandier's death, apparently of extreme physical and mental stress. The surgeon who had found Grandier's supposed Devil's marks died soon also—after seeing Grandier's ghost. Two of the exorcists became possessed before the horror ended. One of them died largely because of the strain, and the other had a complete mental and physical breakdown that lasted for several years.

Grandier's execution, with demons—or pigeons—flying above the flames.

What happened at Loudun could be called an epidemic. Similar epidemics were reported elsewhere in France in the sixteenth and seventeenth centuries, and also in Holland, Italy, Germany, and Spain. Why? You can find a clue in another case—this time in Berry, Alabama, in 1973. Right—1973.

The Alabama case took place in a school, not a convent, and was not, in this modern age, called "possession," but nevertheless its events fall into a somewhat similar pattern. According to Martin Ebon, author of *The Devil's Bride, Exorcism: Past and Present*, the *Wall Street Journal* reported the case in November 1973, saying that the trouble began when a girl in the fifth grade scratched a rash she was suffering from. She scratched so vigorously her teacher asked her to leave the room. For a while everything was fine, but then other students in the same class started scratching, and soon students in other classes were scratching too. Within a few hours, the school had an epidemic on its hands. By that time, it was no longer simple scratching. Some students actually felt sick, with stomachaches, nausea, and sore throats. A few fainted and many cried and moaned. The school had to send seventy of them to the hospital.

At first, school officials thought some kind of poison must have gotten into the air or water. Then they wondered if a tiny unseen insect could have attacked the students. But it turned out neither of those was the explanation. It turned out to be a simple—or maybe not so simple—case of hysteria.

How exactly does that sort of thing happen? The power of suggestion has a lot to do with it. If you think hard enough about, say, having an itch on your right arm, chances are your arm will actually feel itchy before very long. If you see a friend scratching and think about how itchy he or she must feel, you may feel itchy too. Multiply that many times by many people, and add the panic it causes as the affliction spreads with no one knowing why, and you'll have an idea of how a simple suggestion can get out of control and lead to hysteria—rather like a severe case of the giggles but worse.

Something like that, modern psychologists think, is probably what happened at Loudun and in other convents. It is probably also what led to a sudden increase in possession scares in the United States after the release of the movie *The Exorcist*. In some cases of possession—Loudun is probably one of them—even the person trying to drive the demons away can be responsible for aggravating or even causing the victim's symptoms by talking about and therefore suggesting them. The same thing can happen when a person sees a vivid portrayal of possession, as in *The Exorcist*. And, in close quarters like a school or convent, one person's symptoms can easily suggest symptoms to others. That doesn't mean the students in Alabama or the nuns at Loudun were faking. Hysterical people truly cannot control their actions, just as people with psychosomatic illnesses really feel sick.

Of course there are also physical diseases—genuine ones—that have been mistaken for demonic possession. The main one is epilepsy, a disease which has many forms and symptoms. Its victims have periodic seizures or "fits" in which their behavior often is identical to the behavior of people said to be possessed. The twitching limbs, protruding tongues, rolled-up eyes, and unconsciousness characteristic of some epileptic seizures are frightening to observe and experience—and, until fairly recent times, people had no idea what caused them. Some epileptics were considered insane and some bewitched. And so many were considered possessed that it is likely that many if not most possession cases recorded before modern times were actually cases of epilepsy.

The simplest explanation for a case of demonic possession, however, came in early Christian times when a woman became possessed after eating a lettuce leaf. The explanation: there was a demon sitting on the leaf at the time! Later, witches were occasionally accused of causing possession by putting demons into apples or other food, but more often, like Grandier, they were believed to use more mysterious means. Most instances of possession, however, were believed to occur without the aid of a go-between. The person simply became possessed because a demon chose to take over his or her body.

Once in a while, even in the old days, people realized that victims of possession had some kind of illness—but they usually thought that all the illness was responsible for was weakening the victim and making it easier for a demon to enter. Modern parapsychologists tend to believe that few cases of possession are genuine and that those that are usually involve spirits of the dead rather than demons. Many psychiatrists and other doctors, however, doubt there is any such thing as true demonic possession and say that usually "possessed" people are in some way mentally ill or disturbed. Sometimes, say psychiatrists, possession can be the result of extreme guilt. One of the first psychiatrists to study possession scientifically and to find this kind of pattern was Dr. Pierre Janet, who practiced in France at around the turn of the century.

One of Dr. Janet's most famous cases was that of a man in his early twenties whom he referred to in his reports as "Achille," not wishing to publicize his real name. Dr. Janet began treating Achille in 1890.

The patient, according to Dr. Janet, was a man of little education, married, with one daughter; he owned and ran a small business. He'd always been perfectly normal until one day when he came home from a business trip so badly depressed he could hardly speak. In only a few days he actually was unable to talk. Achille saw a couple of doctors, who told him he was physically quite ill. This shocked him enough to enable him to speak again, but his depression grew worse and after a time he said he felt something terrible was going to happen. Then he kissed his wife and daughter as if he were leaving them, and lay down as if dead. For two days he lay on his bed without moving and then, suddenly, he sat up and laughed steadily for two hours, while his whole body shook.

From that day on, Achille acted like a different man. His room, he said, was full of imps and the Devil himself was inside him. He blasphemed and told everyone it was the Devil talking; he had convulsions so terrible he cried out in agony. He was possessed, he said, as a punishment for not being religious enough.

After Achille had made several suicide attempts, his family took him to a Paris hospital, the Salpêtrière, where Dr. Janet practiced under the famous psychiatrist, Jean Martin Charcot. Charcot assigned the case to Janet.

Janet knew that Achille's situation looked exactly like a classic case of demonic possession, but he didn't believe the Devil or any demon was at the root of it. He tried many ways to get Achille to talk to him, including hypnosis and consultations with a priest, but nothing had any effect. Then, more or less by accident, he discovered that Achille would answer questions in writing. From then on, Dr. Janet gave Achille pencil and paper whenever he questioned him. Achille—or the Devil, using Achille's hand—wrote the answers freely. By phrasing his questions very carefully, Dr. Janet got the "Devil" to send Achille into a hypnotic sleep. In this state, Achille revealed that he was feeling horribly guilty for something he'd done wrong—Dr. Janet doesn't say what in his report of the case—on his business trip. Achille was afraid to tell anyone, especially his wife, what he'd done and had tried to forget about it, but instead he'd thought about it night and day. He felt he deserved to be punished and had convinced himself that something dreadful was going to happen to him as a result of his great sin. During the two days on which he'd acted dead, Dr. Janet deduced, Achille's tortured mind had told him he really was dead. When he'd woken up with that terrible laugh, he'd thought the Devil had taken his soul.

Achille's illness, said Dr. Janet, was guilt, not demonic possession. Eventually he was able to convince Achille that his wife forgave him for whatever it was he'd done wrong—and that was the end of Achille's "possession."

The fact that psychiatrists like Dr. Janet have found that demonic possession can be confused with hysteria, extreme stress, epilepsy, or mental illness does not mean that no one believes in it anymore. People who believe firmly in the Devil and his powers usually also believe in possession—and, as a speech made by Pope Paul VI in 1972 shows, people certainly still do believe in the Devil. In his speech, Pope Paul said the Devil is "a living spiritual being" and "the enemy number one." Although many liberal Catholics disagreed with him, other Catholics did not. And in June 1975, an article in *l'Osservatore Romano*, the Vatican newspaper, spoke of "the existence of the devil's world," calling it "a fact of dogma." Both the Catholic Church and the Protestant Anglican Church (Church of England) still practice the rite of exorcism when called upon to do so and when convinced that a possession case is genuine.

The job of exorcist is not one that is taken lightly. Because of the work of Dr. Janet and others like him, Church authorities are the first to admit that any case of possession must be approached with extreme care and even with skepticism. Many other things, they realize, can seem to be possession, both to the victim and to the victim's family and friends. An exorcist, says the Church, must first be able to tell whether a case of possession is real or pretended, and second whether it is due to demonic possession or some natural cause.

But it's often hard to tell. Unless the victim speaks or understands a language he or she doesn't know, there's no sure test. A reasonably good one, however, involves sacred objects: if the victim is "burned" by holy water, for example, there's a good chance, says the Church, that the possession is real. But even this test must be performed with great caution. The most reliable technique is to announce to the possessed that one is going to use holy water, and then use ordinary water instead. Naturally someone who is faking or who is not truly possessed will cry out, "Stop, stop, it's burning me!" A demon, on the other hand, will know the difference and will say so immediately.

Exorcists should, say Church authorities, have a thorough enough knowledge of mental and physical illness to know when to call in a doctor to examine the victim. They are urged to do this especially when they suspect hysteria, for a hysterical person can easily be "cured" by an exorcist who makes the right suggestions, but will just as easily fall back into fits again and again afterward, as did the nuns at Loudun.

The usual technique, followed by exorcists since the days of ancient Egypt, is to address the demon directly and order him to depart. There have been occasional variations, however. Early Jewish exorcists recited the names of angels in order to cast out demons; sometimes they used herbs for the same purpose. In the Middle Ages, possessed people were sometimes beaten, or twirled around and around on a wheel to make the demons fly out. By the fifteenth century, there were traveling exorcists in Europe, not always connected with the Church, who apparently used whatever methods they liked, including whipping. But as early as 1583, the Church recognized that possession was not always what it seemed to be. The Acts of the National Synod of Rheims declared in that year that some insane or deeply unhappy people mistakenly believed themselves to be possessed and declared that people like that were "more in need of a doctor than of an exorcist."

In 1614 the Catholic Church, under Pope Paul V, published a document called the *Rituale Romanum*, which gives complete instructions for performing exorcisms. The *Rituale* was revised slightly in 1952, but it is basically the same today as it was back then. It is the *Rituale* which urges exorcists to study cases carefully to make sure they are genuine. Exorcists must, say the *Rituale*, always apply to a bishop for permission to perform an exorcism; exorcists must be truly religious, well-prepared, skillful, and objective, and must conduct all ceremonies with dignity—which lets out public spectacles like those at Loudun. The struggle, according to the *Rituale*, is not a personal one between the exorcist and the demon (as it often seemed to be at Loudun), but one between God or Christ and the demon; the exorcist is only a humble intermediary.

The main part of the exorcism rite in the *Rituale* consists of commands to the demon to leave. The demon is asked to leave without harming anyone and to return, forever, to the place from which he or she came. The exorcist prays before and after each command, reads from the Bible, makes the sign of the cross, uses holy water. Sometimes he asks St. Michael the archangel for assistance. He addresses the demon as "unclean spirit," "evil spirit," and similar names; he calls Satan names like "Old Serpent" and "enemy of the human race." Sometimes he asks the demon questions, but only when it seems absolutely unavoidable; the point is not to argue or discuss, but to command.

The Anglican rite is similar to the one described in the *Rituale Romanum*. In 1971 the Right Reverend Robert Mortimer, Bishop of Exeter, joined with other British clergymen, some Catholic and some Protestant, to work out a modern system of exorcism for the Church of England. The bulk of this ritual consists of a short prayer in which "every evil spirit" is ordered to leave the victim without causing any harm and is told to "return to the place appointed you, there to remain forever." Like the *Rituale Romanum*, the bishop's report stresses the importance of careful diagnosis and says that the exorcist must be experienced and must act only with the permission of his bishop.

There have been exorcists, of course, all over the world and in many, many religions. Jewish rabbis cast out dybbuks, who were more apt to be spirits of dead people than demons; Puritan ministers cast out Satan. One of the best-known non-Catholic exorcisms was that of the demons who tormented a young German girl, Gottliebin Dittus, in the 1840s. Her exorcist was a Lutheran pastor.

There was very little joy in young Gottliebin's life when she first suffered from possession in 1841, an affliction that was to remain with her till her pastor, Johann Cristoph Blumhardt, conquered it in 1843. Gottliebin's mother had told her many times that as a baby Gottliebin had twice disappeared from her side when she was sleeping—and had only appeared again, on the floor, when her mother had cried out to Jesus for help. Pastor Blumhardt, who described Gottliebin's case in great detail,° pointed out that super-

---

° Frank S. Boshold, trans. *Blumhardt's Battle*. New York: Thomas E. Lowe, Ltd., 1970.

stitious people in Gottliebin's village believed that sorcerers stole small children in order to teach them magic. If Gottliebin knew that superstition, it is easy to see that from an early age she might have been worried that she had been in some way singled out by supernatural forces. It also can't have helped her mental health any to have had an older cousin hint to her that she, Gottliebin, was destined for "great things"—and then die before she was able to explain what they were.

Gottliebin was not a very strong person physically either. When she was in her early twenties, she was ill for two years with a kidney disease. Even when she was pronounced well, she still had unpleasant problems with her digestion as a result of the disease and also, for some reason, she had a short foot. Soon after her "recovery," she was left an orphan and had to move into an apartment with her two sisters and her half-blind brother. The four were so poor that they often had trouble buying enough to eat.

At about this time, Gottliebin had some strange experiences with money. Once, she was sure, some extra coins appeared in her hand when she was on her way with her last bit of small change to buy some milk. She threw the coins away, thinking they came from the Devil—but when she got home, there were more coins in her room! Another time she found, inexplicably, some flour and a single coin in the living room of the apartment. Perhaps she did not remember that she had extra money; perhaps someone else put the flour in the living room; perhaps she imagined what she saw—or perhaps she even stole the extra money and the flour without being aware of it. Whatever the reason, these events, mysterious to Gottliebin, troubled her deeply.

Gottliebin's first fit of possession occurred while grace was being said at a meal soon after she had moved into the apartment: she fainted. There followed a chain of events very like a poltergeist haunting. The whole family was disturbed at night by banging sounds in various rooms of the apartment. Gottliebin sometimes felt that something unseen was making her fold her hands; she began to see ghostly figures. Then she got physically sick again, this time with a disease called erysipelas, a contagious skin infection which, since it is accompanied by a fever, may have exaggerated her other problems. After a two months' bout with that illness, Gottliebin still saw ghosts, most frequently the ghost of a local woman two years dead, with a dead child in her arms. Other strange things happened too. A piece of paper mysteriously appeared one night with something written on it that no one could read. Another night a light suddenly glowed near the stove, and when the family investigated, they found a box containing salt, bones, chalk, and other small objects. There were trampling sounds at night, and more coins appeared. Gottliebin continued to see the woman's ghost.

Finally someone suggested that the ghost was restless because in life she had killed the child she carried; perhaps she kept returning to this particular house because the child was buried there. Well, that seemed easy enough to check. After a certain amount of digging, someone unearthed a number of small bones from under the house—bones which a local gravedigger said were clearly those of a child. But the medical examiner disagreed. "They're the bones of a bird," he said—so that was the end of that theory.

At this point, Pastor Blumhardt, who had been stopping in to give advice every now and then, had Gottliebin moved to another house, and for a while things were quiet. But soon the old tramplings and bangings started in the new house, and now, whenever she heard them, Gottliebin either went rigid or had a convulsion. By the summer of 1842, her convulsions were so bad they twisted her body into seemingly impossible contortions. No mortal person, Blumhardt thought, watching her, could twist and turn that way without breaking bones and tearing muscles, unless . . . unless that person were possessed.

As soon as that occurred to him, Blumhardt tried acting as Gottliebin's exorcist and, as often happens in such cases at first, the situation rapidly got out of control. Gottliebin's convulsions eased when Pastor Blumhardt prayed, but afterward they returned worse than before. She complained of seeing the ghost and other "shapes"; Blumhardt said that some kind of "spiritual power" came from her fingers. Soon Blumhardt, like some of the exorcists at Loudun, began suffering from some of his victim's symptoms; he heard, for example, the same mysterious sounds Gottliebin did.

At last Blumhardt questioned the ghost, using Gottliebin as an intermediary. The ghost told him she had killed two children and that the Devil was with her. Gottliebin's symptoms changed after the ghost's confession. One by one, according to Blumhardt, fourteen demons "came out" of her and her face changed its appearance with each one. Gottliebin—or the demons—threatened Blumhardt; Gottliebin tore her hair and banged her head against the wall. Each time, when Blumhardt prayed over her and ordered the demons to leave, she calmed down temporarily. But the demons kept returning, stronger and more horrible than before. Their number went from 14 to 175 to 425 and finally to 1,067! During this process Gottliebin tried to kill herself and had several unexplained hemorrhages during which she bled so badly that doctors could not see how she survived. Bruises and wounds appeared on her body though no one knew how they got there. She vomited coins, nails, and a tin box that had been in the pocket of a garment hanging in her room. Similar objects, said Blumhardt, came out through the skin on various parts of her body.

By Christmas 1843, Gottliebin had grown a little calmer, but Pastor Blumhardt still had his hands full, for her affliction had spread to her brother and one of her sisters. The sister, whose name was Katharina, had a demon who claimed that he wasn't the spirit of a dead person, as were many of Gottliebin's demons, but a servant of Satan himself. Katharina had a worse time, in a way, than Gottliebin; at least she screamed and fought and blasphemed as if she did. (She also remembered everything afterward, which is unusual in possession cases.) But at last, with a great and horrible roar, so loud that Blumhardt was sure it could be heard by nearly everyone in the village, Katharina's demon left—screeching "Jesus is victor" as it went.

And that, essentially, was that! It must have seemed anticlimactic after such a long time and such a terrible struggle. Gottliebin and Katharina had a couple of fits after Katharina's big Christmas one, but nothing as bad as their previous ones, and it was not long before even those stopped. Gottliebin was completely restored to health— even the digestive complications left over from the kidney disease disappeared. She also found some measure of happiness, it seems, for she moved in with Blumhardt's family to do housework and help his wife care for their children. Before long she was also helping Blumhardt minister to mentally ill people, with whom, he said, she was especially helpful.

Gottliebin's case happened fewer than one hundred and fifty years ago; Douglass Deen's, fewer than fifty. Even so, we can't be certain whether or not they were genuine. We do know, however, that most of the really recent cases, those prompted by *The Exorcist*, probably were not. One Catholic priest, Richard Woods, author of a book called *The Devil*, said that in a recent six-month period he was asked by seven different people to perform exorcisms and was called by many others for advice related to possession. Of the seven, said Woods, at least four had been influenced by *The Exorcist*. None of the seven people, he said, was truly possessed.

Other clergymen made similar statements during the first few months of 1974, soon after *The Exorcist* was released. Many people, they said, felt they were possessed at around that time, but turned out not to be. A Harris poll taken during that period found that 36 percent of the people in the United States thought people could be possessed, and 53 percent believed in the Devil. It's easy to see, with so many twentieth-century people believing in possession, possibly influenced by a movie, how the poor sisters of Loudun suffered from possession hysteria for so long!

Ah, but none of them—no one in this book, in fact—seems to have known about Brother Juniper. If more people down through the ages had known about him, everyone might have been saved a lot of pain and fear. No one seems to know exactly what his secret was, but this good monk, according to St. Francis, so terrified demons that all one had to do was mention his name and poof! Demons would fall all over themselves and one another to "return to the place they came from." It seems the first demon Brother Juniper dealt with was too frightened even to leave his victim, so he ran, in the body of the exhausted possessed man, literally miles before anyone could catch up with him long enough to exorcise him. Word of whatever it was Brother Juniper had done to him must have spread rapidly through hell, for from then on, according to St. Francis, all an exorcist really had to do was threaten to call Brother Juniper and everyone's possession troubles would vanish like magic.

Who knows? If he'd been born early enough, good old Brother Juniper might even have been able to vanquish the Terrible Seven!

Suggestions for Further Reading

MOST OF THE DEVIL STORIES in this book are legends and folktales, not stories made up by writers. But the Devil's character has so fascinated writers that they have produced a great many wonderful stories about the Fiend in all his guises. One of the best known of these is "The Devil and Daniel Webster" by Stephen Vincent Benét. This and many other devil stories can be found in short story anthologies—and since the same story, if it's famous enough, may be published in several anthologies, the best way to find these gems is by going to the card catalog in your school or public library. Look up "Devil" or ask the librarian for help in finding stories about the Devil; look up "Demons" also—and don't forget to try "Occult" and "Supernatural." You know how tricky Old Scratch is; you may have to hunt for him a little, even in the library.

And, while you're at it, here are some other books for you to look for, about the Devil, demons, and related subjects.

Arabian Nights Entertainments. There are many versions of these wonderful old tales. You might try the paperback edited by Andrew Lang, published by Dover Publications, New York, 1969.

Appel, Benjamin. *Man and Magic.* New York: Pantheon Books, 1966.

Ashton, John. *The Devil in Britain and America.* San Bernardino: Newcastle Publishing Co., 1972.

Aylesworth, Thomas G. *Servants of the Devil.* Reading, Mass.: Addison-Wesley Publishing Co., 1970.

Boyd, Mildred. *Man, Myth and Magic.* New York: Abelard-Schuman, 1969.

Causley, Charles, ed. *The Puffin Book of Magic Verse.* Baltimore: Penguin Books, 1974.

Cohen, Daniel. *Magicians, Wizards & Sorcerers.* Philadelphia: J. B. Lippincott Co., 1973.

Garden, Nancy. *Witches*. Philadelphia: J. B. Lippincott Co., 1975.

Gregor, Arthur S. *Witchcraft and Magic*. New York: Charles Scribner's Sons, 1972.

Haining, P. H. *Witchcraft and Black Magic*. New York: Bantam Books, 1973.

Hearn, Lafcadio. *In Ghostly Japan*. Rutland, Vt.: Charles E. Tuttle Co., 1971.

Hoyt, Olga. *Demons, Devils and Djinn*. New York: Abelard-Schuman, 1974.

Hunter, Mollie. *Thomas and the Warlock* (fiction). New York: Funk & Wagnalls Publishing Co., 1967.

Hyatt, Victoria, and Charles, Joseph W. *The Book of Demons*. New York: Simon & Schuster, 1974.

Kelen, Betty. *Gautama Buddha, in Life and Legend*. New York: Lothrop, Lee & Shepard Co., 1967.

Knight, David C. *Poltergeists: Hauntings and the Haunted*. Philadelphia: J. B. Lippincott Co., 1972.

Manning-Sanders, Ruth. *A Book of Devils and Demons*. New York: E. P. Dutton & Co., 1970.

McHargue, Georgess. *Impossible People: A History Natural and Unnatural of Beings Terrible and Wonderful*. New York: Holt, Rinehart and Winston, 1972.

Olcott, Henry S. *People from the Other World*. Rutland, Vt.: Charles E. Tuttle Co., 1972.

Preussler, Otfried. *The Satanic Mill* (fiction). Translated by Anthea Bell. New York: Macmillan Publishing Co., 1973.

Selden, George. *The Genie of Sutton Place* (fiction). New York: Farrar, Straus & Giroux, 1973.

Shecter, Ben. *Game for Demons* (fiction). New York: Harper & Row, Publishers, 1972.

Wedeck, Harry E. *Treasury of Witchcraft*. Secaucus, N. J.: Citadel Press, 1966.

Index